REWRITING LOVE STORIES

Brief Marital Therapy

REWRITING LOVE STORIES

Brief Marital Therapy

WITHDRAWN

Patricia O'Hanlon Hudson

William Hudson O'Hanlon

W.W. NORTON & COMPANY   New York • London

Printed in the United States of America.

The text of this book is composed in Garamond Book. Composition
by Bytheway Typesetting Services, Inc. Manufacturing by Haddon
Craftsmen, Inc.
Book design by Justine Burkat Trubey.

Library of Congress Cataloging-in-Publication Data

Hudson, Patricia O'Hanlon.
  Rewriting love stories : brief marital therapy / Patricia O'Hanlon
Hudson and William Hudson O'Hanlon.
    p.   cm.
  "A Norton professional book"—Half t.p.
  Includes bibliographical references and index.
  ISBN 0-393-70125-5
  1. Marital psychotherapy. 2. Brief psychotherapy. I. O'Hanlon,
William Hudson. II. Title.
RC488.5.H826   1992
616.89'156—dc20   91-28422   CIP

W. W. Norton & Company, Inc. 500 Fifth Avenue, New York, N.Y. 10110
W. W. Norton & Company Ltd., 10 Coptic Street, London WC1A 1PU

    2   3   4   5   6   7   8   9   0

Lovingly dedicated to our children, Angie, Nick, and Zack Hexum and Patrick O'Hanlon, and to R. Lofton Hudson, who continues, at age 81, to inspire us as a therapist and parent.

To Pat who has rewritten my love story.

—Bill

To Bill for being the co-author of my love story.

—Pat

ACKNOWLEDGMENTS

Thanks to our friends and colleagues, Lofton Hudson, Julie Jurich, Liz Kofoed, Sandy Kutler, Mary Neumann, and Karen Stacey for comments on the manuscript.

Thanks to the couples with whom we have worked who have so freely shared their stories, their laughter, and their pain, and who helped teach us how to be marital therapists.

Thanks to our editor, Susan Barrows, who has always been so encouraging and who suggested that we write this book.

CONTENTS

Chapter 10
WHY SHOULD YOUR VAGINA BE DIFFERENT
FROM YOUR EAR?: Intimacy and Sex

Chapter 11
RELATIONSHIP GLUE: Eliciting Love and
Commitment

REWRITING LOVE STORIES

Brief Marital Therapy

INTRODUCTION

Let's clear up something right from the start. People are sometimes baffled by our names, Patricia O'Hanlon Hudson and William Hudson O'Hanlon. They wonder if we are siblings, or perhaps it's just an amazing coincidence! Yes, we are married. When we married Bill took Pat's family name as his middle name and Pat took his family name as her middle name.

Pat is the executive director of a private counseling center, the Hudson Center, which she co-founded in 1975 with her father, Dr. Lofton Hudson. Lofton was an early pioneer in pastoral counseling (he is a Southern Baptist minister) and had written one of the first books on marital counseling (Hudson, 1963). Her father's work has had a big influence on Pat's approach to therapy, so Pat can say she definitely comes by her interest in and knowledge of marital therapy honestly. Pat has also experienced first-hand the ineffectiveness of much of the marital counseling available. When she was having serious difficulties in her previous marriage, she sought help from prominent thera-

1

pists in several states in the Midwest. Pat was divorced in 1983.

Bill came to this book through personal and professional routes. In his personal life, he was very shy and had a history of terrible relationships. After seeing (and experiencing) so many ways that relationships didn't work, he became interested in finding out what made relationships work. He developed some simple ideas that he began using in his own relationships. He found that these ideas made quite a big difference. He then began applying these ideas with couples he worked with in marital/couple therapy. Many of his clients achieved good results using these ideas, so he decided to teach them to the general public, hoping to help people improve their relationships and avoid unnecessary misery and divorce. The class was called "Love is a Verb." Soon Bill was teaching the class for community groups on a regular basis and refining the ideas.

Pat and Bill became professional colleagues and friends after Bill moved to Omaha in the early 1980s. In 1982, Pat asked Bill to join the Hudson Center staff. He accepted. Pat heard Bill's "Love is a Verb" class and became quite intrigued with the ideas. She started to use them with her clients and found them easy to implement and quite helpful in therapy. As she jokes, she liked the class so much that she decided to marry Bill so she could teach it with him. In 1985, Bill and Pat were married. Together we have four children, ranging in age (at the time this is being written, in mid-1991) from 5 to 23. Pat, still director of the Hudson Center for Brief Therapy in Omaha, is Bill's boss.

We teach these ideas around the world (so far, in the U.S., Australia, Asia, Europe, South America, Canada and Mexico) and have found acceptance and interest in them even in different cultures. In relationships it seems, to echo Harry Stack Sullivan, that we are all simply more human than otherwise.

Having taught these ideas and methods many times, we are used to a few common concerns. The first is that these ideas are very simple. Some people think that they are too simple. It *must* be more complicated or deeper than this. We have tried to make things as simple and clear as possible without, in our view, oversimplifying. We are adamant about keeping it this simple because we find so often that therapists get lost in arcane and complex theories that keep them from helping solve the urgent concerns that bring people for relationship counseling. While no book can adequately address the complexities of people's lives, we think that this model is open enough to deal with diverse situations. For some, the simplicity of the model may be offputting, but for most the clear map we have offered will, we hope, prevent their getting bogged down in the swamplands of couples' problems.

The other comment we often hear is that this model seems like a behavioral model. While some of the ideas and methods are compatible with some things that behaviorists do, it is not a behavioral model. We use the word "action" rather than "behavior" to help highlight this distinction. The first difference is that we do not believe in behavioral theory. It seems to us barely applicable to rats and certainly not adequate to deal with couples' relationship problems. In fact, we are opposed to holding any fixed explanatory model for the work we do. We are much more interested in solutions than in explanations (see O'Hanlon & Wilk, 1987; O'Hanlon & Weiner-Davis, 1989). Our work is in the solution-oriented, rather than explanation-oriented, camp.

The other difference between this approach and behaviorism is that we place ourselves in a tradition that includes narrative and constructivist/contructionist views. Our title emphasizes this narrative tradition. We are interested in changes in meanings as well as changes in actions.

Couples come to us with views that have been influenced by their social/familial interactions and language-based constructions of their situations. We are attempting to enter into those constructed views and to influence them in certain directions. Couples have written certain love stories; we help them rewrite those stories.

In addition, some have told us that our ideas resemble cognitive therapy approaches, reality therapy, Ericksonian therapy, or strategic therapy. We have certainly been influenced by many of those approaches, but really this model is just what we do in therapy. We have little interest in placing it within any grand theoretical orientation. We are much more pragmatic than that. This approach has evolved over many years as our way to make the sometimes confusing and difficult work with couples manageable.

We approached this book with a little trepidation. We had heard about former U.S. First Lady and President Rosalyn and Jimmy Carter having terrible rows during their joint writing project. While writing a very early version of this book, Bill once became upset at the inaccurate way Pat was portraying the model. He said heatedly, "You can put that in there if you don't mind being wrong!" Pat responded, "I don't mind being wrong as long as we do it my way!" That became our joke for a long time: Bill got to be right as long as we did it Pat's way. Several versions later we had found a way to satisfy us both—a way in which no one had to be right or wrong. Happily, it turned out to be easier than we thought.

We use these ideas on a daily basis in our counseling and personal lives. While they do not work to solve every relationship problem (we don't know any method or technique that does that), they have proven useful to us and to our clients. We offer these ideas to therapists in the hope that they will find them as useful and empowering as we do.

1

CLARITY BEGINS AT HOME
Escape from Blame and Invalidation

The problem with traditional approaches to couples counseling is that they take too long. Most couples seek counseling as a desperate last resort. It is as if they are saying, "We're on our way to divorce court, but we thought we ought to stop by here for a few minutes just to see if there were anything you could do."

There is no time to delay in these situations. No time, in our view, to learn about problems in each partner's parents' or grandparents' lives that might have some resemblance to the couple's problems. No time to have them free associate about their childhoods for months or years to get to the root of the problem. Most people's marriages* won't last that long in crisis. If they do last, they

---

*We use the word "marriage" as a shorthand term for any committed romantic/sexual relationship, realizing that many such relationships are

could be severely damaged by the years of problems that ensue or continue.

In this book we offer a model for doing marital therapy briefly. The brevity of this approach does not mean, however, that we do crisis counseling with couples. Although couples are usually in crisis when they seek marital therapy, the therapy we offer is not a "patch up" or designed merely to get them over the immediate crisis. The brief therapy described here is intended to bring about lasting changes.

Many traditional approaches to marital therapy often add to the couple's problem by replicating some of the very processes that are part of the couple's problems in the first place. In therapy, discussions can revolve around things like attributing blame and fixed labels to people, guessing at motives, and speculating that the "real" issue is not the one being talked about. These discussions are similar to the way couples discuss things with one another at home. We want to do something new, not more of the same.

Beyond Blame, Invalidation, and Explanations

Few people thrive in an atmosphere of blame. Yet, advertently or inadvertently, that's the atmosphere that is often created by therapists dealing with marital problems. A prime example of this kind of thinking is found in self-help books designed to help couples solve their

---

not formal marriages (e.g., gay/lesbian relationships). This model applies just as well to those "non-traditional" relationship forms, although there may, of course, be issues that are unique to them.

relationship problems. Most of these books are written by therapists and are derived from traditional therapy models.

Self-help books on relationships are typically about diagnosing the relationship or one's partner. Look at the shelves in the bookstore under "psychology" or "self-help" and you'll find books that diagnose men as haters of women, women as masochistic or codependent, men as dance-away lovers, afraid of intimacy, etc. We think this is a bad trend. At best, it usually doesn't help couples change their relationships in positive directions. At worst, it can add to the problems couples already have.

What are people seeking when they latch onto diagnoses? Our sense is that people are usually seeking acknowledgment and validation for their feelings and perceptions. They want to know that they are not "crazy" for feeling the way they feel or seeing things the way they do. Reading books about what's wrong with other people is like finding out that your neighbors have the same problems that you have. It can give you solace and a sense of being more "normal." And that's fine—as far as it goes. But there are some traps in these schemas that can contribute to relationship problems.

Blaming Does Not Invite
Change and Cooperation

The first trap is the tendency of these diagnoses to sound like blame. When a woman gives her husband *Men Who Hate Women and the Women Who Love Them*, the husband rarely appreciates the gesture. He doesn't say, "Why thanks, honey. I can see that I've got a problem and I need to work on it. You've probably saved me six months of

intensive psychotherapy and I appreciate it.'' No, he usually says something like, ''Get that psychology crap out of
my face. If only you wouldn't analyze our relationship so
much, we'd be okay.''

As wise feminists point out, books like *Women Who
Love Too Much* end up blaming women, as does the concept of codependency. The tradition of blaming women
has a long history, with its roots in psychoanalysis. After
all, who was it that did the feeding and toilet training that
made the oral and anal stages so traumatic? Women. We
don't want either sex to take the bad rap for marriage
problems. Deciding who is the biggest culprit does not
usually help the marriage.

Labels Can Disempower and Stick Like Crazy Glue

Labels can also give the impression that the person is forever doomed to be what the label says he or she is. We call
this ''Hardening of the Categories'' or ''Other-Fulfilling
Prophecies'' (a variation on self-fulfilling prophecies).
Labels are almost always one-dimensional. If you teach
school, you are more than a teacher. You may be a man
or a woman, a skier, a musician, a religious person, and
many other things. The problem is that, once people see
you in that one-dimensional way, it is often difficult for
them to see you in a different light.

We were walking in our city one night and passed a
familiar-looking woman on the street. It took us both a
minute and then we recognized the woman as our son's
preschool teacher. Pat said, ''Hi, Laurie. I guess you have
a life outside of school.'' Laurie smiled and answered,
''Yes, I do.'' Bill was glad Pat had spoken first, because
his impulse, once he recognized her, was to say, ''Hi, Miss
Laurie.'' Laurie was more than a preschool teacher—she

had many other facets to her life—but we had only seen her as *Miss Laurie, the teacher.*

Having a Good Explanation Does Not Necessarily Produce Change

The third trap is that these diagnoses can lead the focus away from change and into explanation. One pundit put it this way, "In life, explanations are the booby prize. They're what you get when you don't get what you want." Unfortunately, clients often settle for explanations over change.

> Bill was doing marriage counseling with a woman and asked her, "What would you like your husband to do differently in your relationship?" She responded, "Well, he was raised in a family of five boys." Bill found it hard to relate her answer to the question, until she explained that she knew it wasn't possible for her husband to give her what she needed, because she knew that being raised in a family of five boys had left him impaired. She wanted him to be more physically affectionate, doing things like holding her hand and putting his arm around her. She had read somewhere that men in general were not very good at expressing affection physically—especially if they were raised in families in which little touching occurred. She believed that he was incapable of doing what she wanted him to do. Bill did not think the man's muscles were unable to reach out and touch her. In fact, when questioned more closely, she revealed that he *had* touched her more when they first dated and during the early part of their marriage. It was not that difficult to get him to touch her more. Her explanation had been part of the problem.

Psychological/Genetic/ Historical/Sociological Determinism

We don't believe that people are determined by their pasts or by biology. We obviously wouldn't be doing "talk" therapy with people if we thought they had unchangeable biological or genetic problems that created their marital difficulties. We do think people are influenced by their pasts and by their genetic and biochemical makeups, but not determined by them.

In addition to advocating biological determinism, some theorists seem to be saying that people are sociologically or historically determined. They grew up with certain circumstances, such as being raised in a certain class or family or having been abused, and therefore they have their current relationship problems. We acknowledge that people's pasts and social contexts have an influence on them but stand firmly against the idea that human beings are determined by their pasts or their social environments.

Relationships can change and can be changed relatively rapidly. We avoid dwelling on people's personalities and the past—not that we never talk about them or that we tell our clients to quit bringing these topics up. It is just that we don't encourage them in these directions, since we think change is likely to happen elsewhere.

The most changeable aspects of the couple's situation, in our view, are in each partner's actions and interpretations of the other's actions. We call this changing the "doing" and the "viewing" of the couple's problem. More on these ideas in future chapters here we want to present the ideas that are the foundation for our model.

Acknowledgment and Validation

Once we were at a party for some of Bill's distant relatives. Pat got into a conversation with a distant cousin of Bill's. When the woman found out Pat was a psychologist and did marriage counseling, she began to tell her of the intimate troubles in her marriage. She told Pat that she was married to a man who hated women, that she herself was codependent and an adult child of an alcoholic and a woman who loved too much. After listening to this litany for some time, Pat told the woman that she was thinking of writing a book called *Women Who Read Too Much*. They shared a laugh about that and the woman said, "I'd probably read that one, too!"

Publishing experts know that it is mostly women who buy these books about relationships. Why? What are they searching for so desperately? They are, in part, searching for some understanding of the unhappy situation in which they find themselves. They are usually searching for some solution to their dilemmas. However, what hooks them into these books so strongly is that they are searching for acknowledgment and validation of the things they have been feeling and perceiving about themselves and their relationships.

Women in this culture are routinely invalidated and their inner experience remains unacknowledged. Men's experiences, of course, also get invalidated, but not nearly as often as women's. For example, if a woman gets angry, someone might ask her if she is having her period. When a male politician refuses to budge on an issue, he is viewed as resolute or stubborn. A woman taking the same stance is seen as cold and uncaring. So women absorb all they can from women's magazines, television, radio, and books about relationships, looking for answers and for validation of their experience.

For us, then, marital therapy must begin with acknowledging each partner's experience and perceptions in the situation. By acknowledging, we don't mean just nodding sagely and saying a few "uh huh's" and "so you feel angry when he does that" kind of thing. We mean an active process of articulating and validating each person's felt experience in the marriage.

We'll get more specific on what this involves, but first let us make a three-part distinction that is crucial to understanding acknowledgment and its part in the change process in therapy.

The Distinction Between Facts, Stories, and Experience

We distinguish between three different aspects of people's situations—the facts, the stories, and experience.

- The *facts* are those aspects of the situation that could be agreed upon by most observers, by consensus. They constitute what you would perceive with your senses in any particular situation.

- The *stories* are the meanings and interpretations we give to those facts. We call them stories to remind the reader (and occasionally our clients) that they are not truths, but theories, constructs and made-up hypotheses.

- *Experience* is the label we use to describe the internal feelings, sensations, fantasies, automatic thoughts and sense of self that each person has.

Just the Facts, Ma'am

There are three ways to know when your clients are sticking to the facts. The first is to use what we call "videotalk."

VIDEOTALK

Videotalk means not going beyond describing what one could see or hear on a videotape about the situation. It is an alternative to using vague words that are open to different interpretations or telling other people one's interpretation of the situation. Videotalk focuses on what the situation looks or sounds like.

While we were writing an earlier version of this book, Pat was two weeks from delivering a baby. Pat and Bill had gone out for dinner. Bill did not talk or touch Pat as much as usual that night. (Bill later confirmed Pat's observation that there had been little talking or touching.) That night, when Pat awoke in the middle of the night, she began to think of all the meanings Bill's actions could have had. It could have meant that he was inwardly focused in anticipation of the birth of his first child; it could have meant that he was feeling somewhat left out of all the excitement around Pat; it could have meant that he found Pat less attractive with her beachball-sized abdomen; it could have been that he was in a more inward mood from having worked on writing a book all day; or it could have been that he was thinking of the duties that would soon be his. Fortunately for Bill, Pat waited until morning to discuss her concerns. She related to him her thoughts and asked him about the meanings of his actions. Frequently, however, in similar situations, people decide they *know* which meaning is correct without considering that other stories could fit the facts. Unfortunately, they usually don't check out their stories with the other person.

The videotalk description of the situation was that Bill was sitting near Pat without talking or touching her. If we were watching a video of that night, we could agree on that part. We might not agree on the meaning of the behavior, however. Some would interpret it one way, and others would be sure that it meant something entirely different.

X = X (NO ADDED MEANINGS)

Another way to state the facts is not to add any meanings to one's description of a situation. The meaning isn't in the thing, the word, or the action. We bring meanings to the situation. You may remember the advertising slogan for the movie "Love Story": "Love is never having to say you're sorry." Well, in facts-land, love is love and never having to say you're sorry is never having to say you're sorry. The difficulty with the movie slogan is that for some people, love means never having to say you're sorry, but for others love means saying you're sorry sometimes. Things become difficult, of course, when someone who thinks love means never having to say you're sorry marries someone for whom love means saying you're sorry.

INCLUDING THE OPPOSITE
POSSIBILITY OF MEANING
(OR NOT)

The last way to state the facts is to include the possibility of the opposite meaning. If you've ever read an article on the warning signs that indicate your spouse is having an affair, you might decide that when he comes home late from work regularly he is having an affair. Well, in facts-land, someone who comes home late from work regularly is either having an affair or he is not. He could be working late. He could be shopping for a surprise present for you; he could be at the bar drinking; or he could be becoming a "workaholic." If you don't know for certain what it means, you are making up stories.

We can even predict the future accurately with this way of talking. "It will either rain today or it won't." There's not much basis for disagreement when you include all the possibilities for meaning in your talk.

The Facts

•   Facts are what can be verified by our senses—what we can see, hear, smell, taste or touch.

•   There are three ways to state the facts:

  1.   Use videotalk. State what it would look and sound like on a videotape.
  2.   Don't add any meanings or interpretations.
  3.   Include the opposite possibilities of meaning ("or not").

Lost in Storyland

Each of us has our own point of view on things that happen in our relationships. We call these points of view "stories." Facts are things we can all agree upon. Facts are what one can see, hear, smell, taste, and touch. Stories involve interpretations, theories, and explanations. Facts are the "what" and stories are the "why."

Stories are part of our ways of understanding the world and what happens in our lives. Each of us puts our experiences together in our own individualized way. We have different maps for the same terrain. One person might be looking at a topographical map while the other has a road map, yielding very different views—yet the territory remains the same.

We each use stories to explain what happens in our relationships and to guess at the future. When there are problems or when people disagree, it often becomes a matter of "dueling stories." Whose story is right and whose is wrong? Neither. Both are explanations that cannot be proved either right or wrong.

Stories aren't just neutral, however. When people get into difficulties, they usually develop stories that don't enhance their relationships. Perhaps out of frustration, anger, or hurt, they come up with stories that poison their relationships. "You just want to control me." "You're just like your mother." "You care for your family more than you care for me." "You're selfish." And so on.

People often become convinced that their stories are the TRUTH, that their map is the territory. They get into arguments about who is right or wrong. In a courtroom, perhaps it is useful to decide who is right or wrong, but in relationships, if one person loses the right/wrong battle, the relationship usually loses. As marital therapists, we are often invited by our clients to be judge and jury. Because we hold that the correct story cannot be determined, we avoid these roles.

When we speak with or observe other therapists, we find that they often come up with stories about clients' motives. For example, the therapist might say, "Of course he got angry. He was embarrassed that you had caught him acting that way and was afraid of your rejection." While this interpretation might fit for the person whose motives or feelings were being guessed about, we often

their partners are not "romantic." This can mean many things—from the man's not doing much touching outside of a sexual context to not sending flowers or not remembering birthdays or anniversaries.

Generalizations involve exaggerating to universals like *always, never, nobody, everybody, all the time.* "Nobody cares about how this house looks but me." "He is never on time." "She's always charging up the credit cards."

One of the wonderful things about generalizations is that, if you can get people to think of one exception, then the generalization is challenged. If the partner was on time once, then "never" does not fit. If she once used cash instead of a credit card, then "always" does not fit. We often tease couples that generalizations like *always, never,* and *nobody* are counseling swear words. If we had an obnoxious game show buzzer in our office, we would hit it when we heard the words *always* and *never* during our marital therapy sessions.

Equivalences involve deciding that a concept is made up of certain elements. "Love is never having to say you're sorry." "I just want her to be a wife—you know, cleaning the house, cooking, taking care of the kids."

Exploring the equivalences that people have for such abstract concepts as love, honesty, support, selfishness, romance, fun, etc., takes up a large part of therapy. Translating these kinds of words into action components is crucial to our model.

Evaluations involve deciding that certain things are right or wrong, good or bad, valuable or worthless. "Why do you watch those stupid shows—they're such junk?" "Your mother is a bad person." "Looking at pornography is wrong."

As therapists we often help couples come to appreciate their differences about values. While there can be compromises in the area of actions, sometimes differences in values, even with changes in actions, do not change. Difficulties often arise when one person forgets that values can differ and assumes his or her values are universal and true and the partner is wrong for not agreeing.

Stories Are Not All Bad

We may be giving the impression that we think that stories are always a source of difficulties, when, in fact, stories can support as much as well as hurt a relationship. Pat's mother, Jessie, was great at making up stories that supported her marriage. If Pat's father was what we considered "grouchy," Jessie might say, "Lofton's tired. He's been working so hard." We are not saying that doing a "storyectomy" is the way to get clients to be happy. Clients will continue to generate stories after our treatment. We just want them to take their stories less seriously or generate ones that support their relationships and help them resolve their conflicts.

Partners usually differ on some of their stories when they arrive at our offices. They are occasionally playing dueling stories, trying to decide or get advice on whose story is better or more valid. Our job is to stay out of the molasses by acknowledging each person's story and gently challenging and changing their stories, so they can develop a new one (with a happier ending, or at least a better next chapter).

Acknowledgment
and Challenge

There is an old story about a policeman coming upon a drunk crawling under a streetlight. The policeman asks the man what he is doing and he replies in a slur, "I lost my keys and I'm looking for them." The policeman decides to help the man. However, when, after quite a bit of searching, they still haven't found the keys, the policeman says, "Wait. Let's retrace your movements when you lost the keys. Where exactly were you when you dropped them?" The drunk pointed across the street to a dark corner. The policeman, frustrated, rebuked him. "Why weren't you looking over there for them, then?" The drunk replied, "'Cause there's more light over here."

Like the drunk under the streetlight, most people look in the wrong place when they have lost the keys to love and understanding in their relationships. They most often try to find an explanation for their partner's troubling behavior. The explanation they come up with, on their own or with the help of books, articles, or television shows, usually leads them to conclusions that their partners disagree with and resent. One or both of the partners feel invalidated and/or blamed. Or they might get discouraged because their explanations indicate that change will be impossible.

What we try to do in relationship therapy, then, is to acknowledge each person's experience without trying to change it. We also try to get couples to stop analyzing one another or attempting to change one another's experience or core self. Instead, we focus our (and their) change attempts elsewhere. The elsewhere is on changing actions and changing stories.

In the next chapter, we'll take up the first part of this endeavor, challenging peoples' stories without blaming and invalidating them or their partners.

2

FROM BLAME TO COLLABORATION

Complaints, Requests, and Praise

Once, during a divorce mediation session, we reached a very painstakingly-crafted agreement. The agreement seemed to include all the concerns of each party and had some built-in renegotiation clauses in case of trouble. When we asked the couple how they felt about the agreement, the woman said vehemently, "Bullshit, bullshit, bullshit!" After a moment of stunned silence, Pat ventured, "Could you be a little more specific?" Everyone broke up laughing and we continued the negotiation process.

Couples in conflict typically use vague words and phrases or they use words that blame and close down the possibilities for change. In order to bypass couples' tendencies towards blame and unhelpful analysis, we have developed a simple method for translating blaming, analysis, diagnosis, and vague conversation into language that can help people change more easily. The method is based on what we call "videotalk."

Videotalk involves getting people to translate what they are saying into words that indicate specific actions minus attributed meanings or interpretations. We channel what they say into descriptions that we could see and hear if we were watching a videotape of whatever they are talking about.

When we first started doing couples therapy, people would tell us their ideas about their problems using blaming labels, but often those labels were relatively unsophisticated. "He's a jerk," she would say. "She's a controller," he would counter. We have noticed an increase in psychological sophistication these days. "She's codependent," and "He's passive-aggressive." When Bill hears such talk in his office, he starts sliding his chair away from the man. "Passive-aggressive? I've heard that's nasty stuff, but I'm not sure what it means. Is he doing it now?" Usually the couple laughs. Bill continues, "If he starts doing it during the session, will you let me know?" Then we go on to explore what kinds of things this man has done that she has been calling passive-aggressive and what kinds of things she has done to get the label codependent.

One of the techniques of hypnotic inductions involves using words that are vague and unspecific to give the listener (the trance subject) the freedom to make his or her own interpretations. These words are called "packaged" or "empty" words. They are packaged in the sense that they have many potential meanings packed in them. One must unpack them to find the specific actions and meanings that they involve or suggest. They are empty in the sense that they are devoid of specific meaning. So, packaged or empty words are words that are not specific as to person, place, time, thing, or action. When these vague words are used during a conflict, they often inadvertently induce automatic negative reactions from the listener. What we try to do is interrupt and change these "bad trance" inductions and interactions.

For example, a husband may say to his wife over and over again, "You just can't be close." The wife's eyes may glaze over (a trance-like look) as she withdraws from his words and feels hurt inside. After hearing this often enough, the "just-can't-be-close" phrase becomes like a trance induction.

Another type of "bad trance" induction is the automatic negative reaction that certain phrases, words, or nonverbals evoke from one person. The popular phrase, "That pushed my button," captures this experience well. It is as if someone else holds the remote control that connects directly to one's anger, sense of shame, fear, or hurt. Around Omaha, where we live, there is a strategic air command base, where they have missiles. Some of our clients who work there have taught us the memorable phrase, "I went ballistic when he/she said that."

One of our typical "bad trances" is when Pat says something like, "I'm the only one around here who does anything to clean up the house." This does not get a good response from Bill (who thinks he works quite hard at cleaning the house). He usually "goes ballistic." It does not lead to pleasant or more satisfying interactions for either of us.

While it is fine for hypnotists to use empty or packaged words or for couples to use them in day-to-day interactions, there can be difficulties when the couple is in conflict and these vague, trigger, or blaming words are used. The potential for a hurtful or harmful interpretation to be placed on the words is high.

Instead of allowing couples to continue inducing these bad trances with one another, we invite them into conversations and interactions that lead to more intimacy and closeness. Videotalk is a good way to do this. To enter videotalk, we ask people to make what we call "action complaints" and "action requests" and to give "meaningful praise."

When couples first seek treatment they mainly talk about what they *don't* like about each other. This is not only focused in the past (something that is very difficult to change) but usually, as we've said before, involves blame, mind-reading and vague talk. There is a wonderful Yiddish slang word that captures this kind of talk—it's *kvetching*. Kvetching is difficult to translate precisely, but it generally indicates repetitively complaining about something, nagging and whining in an ineffective manner. Most couples are kvetching. So first we channel their talk into action complaints—complaints that can make a difference.

Action Complaints: From Kvetching to Effecting Change

In order to ensure that people understand one another and to bypass blame and analysis, we coach people to talk about the things they don't like in their relationships in action language (Winograd & Flores, 1987). Complaints involve what has happened in the past that one person does not like or has not liked. We gently channel people's talk about what they dislike in their relationships into videotalk by asking them to get specific. Sometimes we do this very directly, by asking them to give us a recent example. Questions like "What kind of things would I see her doing if she were being inconsiderate?" "When he is acting mean, what is he doing?" "When she embarrassed you, how did she do it? What was she doing?" elicit action complaints and help us move away from vague language (stories).

A woman complained that her husband did not respect her. He disagreed with her conclusion and ar-
gued that he did respect her. When we asked her
for a recent example of her husband showing her
disrespect, she told of an incident at a party when
she had given her political opinion and her husband
had snorted. She had concluded that this indicated
his lack of respect towards her political opinions and,
perhaps, even her right to voice such an opinion. He
confessed that he could not remember snorting on
that occasion, but he admitted that he might have
done it. He agreed not to make noises through his
nose when she was voicing her views.

Sometimes we help people get specific by giving them
multiple choice options in which all the options involve
action descriptions. For example, "When you say he
never listens, do you mean he is usually reading the paper
when you are talking to him, or that he nods when you
tell him something but then doesn't do what you asked him
to do, or that he asks you about something you mentioned
to him before and you think he should have remembered?
Does he do something like that?" Usually, we know enough
about the couple to make a good guess about the videotalk
equivalent of their complaint. Even if we haven't guessed
the right content, we are starting to channel the conversation towards discussing actions rather than vague terms
or reasons. This helps couples get specific.

It is sometimes surprising that people wait until therapy
starts even to mention their complaints.

Pat was working alone with a woman, Deb, who had
already seen an attorney to investigate getting a divorce. She had been married for 18 months and
found several of her husband's habits annoying: she

hated the way he played with the dog, she hated his asking for advice about his clothing in the morning, and she found his way of chewing his food annoying. Pat asked her if she had told her husband these things. Deb responded that she had not. Pat asked why she hadn't. Deb said that she didn't want to hurt his feelings. Pat's eyes got large as she said, "Wait a minute! Let me get this straight. You don't want to hurt his feelings so you are going to divorce him? That will probably hurt his feelings. Maybe you should let him know what you would like changed first." Deb was willing to give him a chance by communicating what she didn't like, so marital therapy could begin.

Action Complaints

Specifying what one partner doesn't like or hasn't liked about the partner's actions.

- Translate empty and packaged words into specifics.

- The listener must be able to see/hear it as if it's on a video.

- Focus on actions, voice tones, voice volumes, facial expressions, gestures, and specific words.

- Help the couple avoid blame, diagnosis, and generalizations.

- Get them to talk about specific incidents.

- Filter out attributions of the other person's intentions or feelings.

One of the first steps may be just getting any complaint, vague or otherwise. The process of moving to actions can then begin and change can occur.

Action Requests

After the complaints have been clarified and specified, it's time to help the couple or the person make some requests. Requests involve one person's asking another to do something new or different in the future or to stop doing something they have done in the past. Again, what distinguishes requests that can make a difference from requests that lead to no change or unproductive arguments is the degree to which the request is stated in videotalk. The request should help the listener understand what actions are to be taken, by whom, and when.

> The woman who felt ridiculed when she voiced her opinions was helped to make an action request to inform her husband how to show her that he respected her. Obviously she wanted him to stop snorting when she voiced her opinions, but was there any action that he could take that would convince her that he respected her? She said one of the ways he might show respect was to stand next to her and hold her hand or make some affectionate physical contact with her during discussions. She said that he usually acted as if he wasn't related to her during parties he would stand far away from her and talk only to others. She would see it as respect if he showed he was connected to her, especially during and after the time she gave her opinion about something. He was surprised by this request, as he hadn't seen mixing with others as a sign of disrespect, and willingly agreed to change his usual style during parties.

At times, one partner will balk at making requests because he or she is convinced the other person is not capable of making the changes that would be requested.

With one couple, Bill had to ask the wife to imagine that she was married to Phil Donahue to get her to articulate what she would like her husband to do. She wanted him to be a "caring listener" to her, but when she was asked what her husband could do to show her that he was a caring listener, she said she could not imagine him doing anything like what she wanted. Phil Donahue, however, would look her in the eye while she was talking and ask her more about what she felt about whatever she was saying.

Helping people make action requests accomplishes another important goal in the treatment: getting people to focus on the future and what they want, rather than on

---

Action Requests

Get the person to tell the partner what would work better than the actions he or she has complained about.

- Avoid requests invoving one person trying to change the other's feelings, attitudes, or personality.

- Get the person who is making the request to get specific about what he or she would like the other person to do or do differently and when he or she would like the other person to do the requested action (in terms of scheduling or specifying frequency).

the past and what they don't want. Sometimes the couple and the therapist get bogged down in the swampland of endless rehashing of the past, with accompanying blame, analysis, and dueling stories. Getting people to talk specifics can help lead out of the swampland onto the road towards solutions and can even give the therapist more hope about the couple's prognosis.

Negotiating Requests

Sometimes, of course, the partners cannot agree about carrying out the requests the therapist has helped them specify. In some cases, one person is just not participating or cooperating in the process. These are usually cases in which one person's behavior is beyond the pale, cases involving drug/alcohol misuse, physical violence, affairs, etc. We will deal with these issues and how to handle one person's lack of cooperation in later chapters. Here we will discuss the situation in which one person has objections to doing the requested actions but is generally willing to cooperate.

There are two typical ways to help people negotiate when one has made a request to which the other has objections. The first is to take the packaged word and find another specific action that would satisfy the request.

One couple had a disagreement about a sexual request. He wanted her to be "more adventuresome" in sex. When we asked for a translation to specific actions, he said he would like her to allow him to have anal intercourse with her. She objected, saying that she had tried it once and it hurt and she found it "too gross." We asked her what other things she thought might be adventuresome that she would be willing to try and she suggested renting an X-rated movie that they could watch together. We then asked him whether that fit his definition of adventuresome. He agreed that it did. He still wanted her to do anal intercourse, but was satisfied with some change that fit with his definition.

The second type of negotiation involves finding the intentions and objections of each person and building them into a workable mutual agreement.

Bob and Lynn had a conflict over how often Bob would call when he was traveling out of town on business. Lynn wanted him to call nightly and he objected, saying that calling so often seemed burdensome to him. Bob was often busy until late in the evening and exhausted when he returned to the hotel. He would often forget to call or be concerned about waking Lynn after she had fallen asleep. He also saw this request as a way for Lynn to try to control him. Lynn said that she wanted to hear from him every night so that she could tell him about important events or to inform him about emergencies or problems with their children. The compromise that we arrived at was that Bob would ensure that he always left the phone number where he was staying or could be reached and Lynn could call him anytime she needed or wanted to talk. If he was too tired to talk, he would merely spend a few minutes checking in with her and then sign off. He also promised to call at least every other day when he was in the country and every three days while overseas.

Meaningful Praise

We would be remiss not to include something on "catching your partner doing something right." It's a tried and true principle of behaviorism, business management, and parenting that it is much more effective to encourage the increase of actions that are already occurring than to try correcting actions that you want to eliminate.

Much of the time, however, when partners are in conflict, they forget to give each other comments and coaching on what's going right. If they do give such comments, they are often given in such vague ways that the other person is not sure why he or she is being praised. Therefore, not much increase in the desired actions occurs.

Meaningful praise, then, is what we propose to remedy this. Like action complaints and requests, meaningfiul praise involves using specifics, videotalk. Instead of letting a comment like, ''I felt really close to you this week,'' pass, we coach the person to tell the partner what, specifically, the other did that helped her develop that feeling of closeness. Bill has told Pat that he's willing to make changes in their relationship if she will let him know what works for her. He asserts that he is a slow learner, but trainable. So Pat has invented a little code phrase that she can use any time she catches Bill doing something right. She just says, ''That's G.H.B., Bill.'' By now, Bill knows that this stands for ''Good Husband Behavior.''

> We were working with Diane and Joe, who started the second session saying that things were just as bad as ever. Pat asked, ''Was that true for the whole two weeks or was there a time that things went better?'' Diane said, ''Things were wonderful for the first five days after our last session.'' Pat seized upon this opportunity by asking what was happening during those first five days. Diane said, ''He was being my companion.'' Pat asked Joe if he knew what it was that Diane called companionship. Joe said that he had done a couple of things: gone shopping with

Diane and taken her out dancing. Pat checked with Diane to be sure that Joe had correctly identified the companionship actions. He had. We emphasized two things: One, that Joe was capable of companionship actions. Two, that if we could keep the ball rolling in that direction, things could improve fairly easily. To help accomplish this, Diane agreed to tell Joe when he was doing "good companionship" actions.

Meaningful Praise

Get each person to specify what he or she liked about what the other person did in the past, between sessions or in a specific situation.

- Get both partners to use videotalk.

- It's okay to talk about general categories, for example, "I like it when you think of me when I'm not around," as long as the listener has enough specific examples to be able to understand what the speaker means.

Videotalk: Antidote to Relationship Poison

This chapter has covered what we consider an essential method that derives from our model: helping people use videotalk to describe specific actions when communicating about conflicts. When couples are in conflict, there is a high probability of misunderstandings and misinterpretations. Usually those misunderstandings are slanted in the direction of blame and invalidation. When enough of these misunderstandings occur, they can and often do poison the relationship. Even when the conflicts are not misunderstandings, the repetition of nonproductive conflicts poisons the relationship. So we offer videotalk, in the form of action complaints, action requests, and meaningful praise, as antidotes to relationship poison. It sometimes amazes us that something so simple as making clear what couples specifically want and don't want can have such a powerfully healing effect on marriages.

3

CHANGING THE "VIEWING" OF THE COUPLE'S SITUATION

In-Session Interviewing Interventions

As we mentioned, there are two general changes that we strive for in brief marital therapy. The first is a change in each person's frame of reference in regard to the problem ("the viewing"). The second change involves altering the actions in the relationship ("the doing"). This chapter presents several methods for bringing about changes in the viewing.

Acknowledging Without Agreeing or Closing Down Possibilities

When partners come to marital therapy, it is often after many arguments, leaving both so frustrated that they feel that no one hears them. In years past therapists focused on creating rapport with clients by ensuring that they felt heard, but more recently that emphasis has been either taken for granted or ignored. Clients need to know that you appreciate their feelings and complaints. If they don't get that sense, they will try all the harder to convince you that their problems and pain are severe, or alternately, they will find someone else who *will* listen to them. Acknowledgment can occur in several ways. Repeating or paraphrasing what the client has said is one of the standard ways to acknowledge that you have heard his or her complaint, feelings, or point of view. Telling a story that shows you understand what he or she is experiencing is another form of validation. If that story contains some "confession" on your part, then hearing it can give the client permission to acknowledge and validate his or her own experience.

"Feeling words" let people know you are sensitive to what they may be experiencing in the marriage. Such phrases as "That was upsetting," "You were hurt by that," or "That must have been frustrating," acknowledge and validate individuals' experiences without making a statement about the wrongness or rightness of their point of view.

Angie and Randy had seen Pat for premarital therapy two years earlier and now returned with stories about Randy's physical abuse of Angie. This had never come out in the premarital therapy. We did several of our typical interventions (marital therapy and hypnosis) and referred Randy to an abusers group.

Angie came in to see Pat alone. Before she came back for therapy Angie had not faced how dangerous and frightening being married to Randy was. They now had a baby and she was feeling trapped. She said she was feeling depressed. Pat said, "That is perfectly understandable. When you came in for therapy you had to face just how scared you had justifiably become in your situation with Randy. I would be down, too.''

Pat was saying in essence, "What you are feeling makes perfect sense." This validated Angie's experience.

Acknowledgment and validation are especially important when one of the partners has been seen alone initially before the couple is seen conjointly.

We were seeing Rob and Jan. They had been married for 13 years. About one year before they came to see us, Jan had surprised herself by starting an affair. In an initial session alone with us, she said that she was amazed that she had had the extramarital relationship because she and Rob had never fought and she felt that she did love Rob. She and Rob had been separated for four months. Jan was enthusiastic about the possibility of turning the separation around by the end of her individual session.

During the second session with Rob and Jan, Pat kept making an effort to let Rob know that he was heard. When he said that this whole situation had hit him like a bolt out of the blue, Pat said, "It really knocked you off your feet for a while," and "You must have been in shock at first." *(She used the past tense to try to encourage seeing the pain as something that had been left behind.)* When Rob poignantly said that he would have been glad to change if he had had any idea that things were going to hurt this much, Pat talked about events in her own life that had changed her from a person who sometimes took a petty perspective to one who focused on loving and caring for the people around her. In the last

three minutes of the session, Jan asked Rob if he felt
ganged up on (not Pat's favorite thing to have asked
with three minutes to go!). Pat held her breath while
she waited for Rob to answer. He said, "Not at all. I
think this has been very helpful."

The main focus of the session had been defining
what actions would be happening if they were "working on the marriage" (which included Jan's agreement
not to see the other man) and planning several activities that would demonstrate that they were moving in
the direction of living together. However, the effort
Pat made to let Rob know that she appreciated his dev-
astation allowed him to feel included and heard. Pat
was careful in this process not to make Jan the villain,
which was probably why she even asked Rob her
"ganged up on" question. Jan felt good about both sessions and obviously did not feel accused by Pat's acknowledgment of Rob's experience.

The process of acknowledging without siding with either partner often involves walking a tightrope, but it is
essential if you are going to get the cooperation of both
partners. We avoid closing down possibilities by siding
with one partner over the other. Sometimes a partner will
ask us, "Wouldn't that have hurt you?" We are good at
seeing both sides of the situation, so we will often answer,
"Yes, that would have hurt me, but I can understand that
your wife's frustration may have led her to such methods." It is imperative that both partners be heard or you
may not have their cooperation in changing the marriage.

Benevolent Skepticism

By now, you know that we are very skeptical about explanations of people's behavior. We call this "benevolent
skepticism." It is "benevolent" because we care about the

couple's relationship too much to let a potential inaccuracy that damages the relationship pass unnoticed. The "skepticism" comes from our view that, in the realm of stories, the scientific truth cannot be known.

> We were working with a couple who were in a blended family. The husband, Tom, was having what could be described as a mid-life crisis. The wife, Terri, was looking for explanations. She thought that perhaps Tom's affair with the woman from work had started when his eight-year-old son had decided to move back with his mother (Tom's first wife). Although Tom agreed that his son's decision had been upsetting, he did not think that caused the affair. Terri then decided that the reason for the crisis was that Tom was still in love with his first wife. He very convincingly denied this explanation as well. Our approach was to tell Terri that it was impossible to know exactly why this affair had happened. Pat told her a story of her own divorce. At the time of her divorce, both Pat and her former husband had thought and even said that they were not sure they had ever loved each other. Years later they had a talk where they both admitted that they had loved each other and that lack of love had not been the reason for the divorce. Their explanations had changed with the passage of time and would probably change again.
>
> We also joked with Terri that if we could do an autopsy on Tom right now it would be impossible to count the neurons in Tom's brain that were "son" neurons, "family of origin" neurons, "first wife" neurons, or "Terri" neurons. She was amused and intrigued by the idea of doing an autopsy on her husband, but accepted that it was not possible to be certain about Tom's reasons. Instead we focused on his

making a commitment to take actions to protect and promote the marriage and to not let his feelings (or anatomy) run the show.

•   •   •   •   •   •

Another couple, Larry and Yvonne, came to an impasse over Larry's view of Yvonne as "negative." We asked for a recent example of Yvonne's being negative. Larry reported that his mother had had dinner plans with them scheduled just before she was to leave with a woman friend to winter in Florida. The mother's friend had broken her foot in the process of preparing for this move. Yvonne suggested that they might call Larry's mom and ask her if she would like to postpone their dinner since she would be taking care of her injured friend. Larry became upset, much to Yvonne's surprise, and said, "Why do you always have to be so negative!?" As we discussed this event, an alternative explanation emerged from our benevolent skepticism. We offered the label of Yvonne as a "caretaker even when caretaking might not be necessary." Larry acknowledged that his explanation of her behavior as "negative" might be wrong.

Casting doubt on stories might be even simpler. If a partner offers the explanation that his partner doesn't love him because she doesn't cook dinner, Pat might say, "I always think Bill is just lazy when he does the same thing!"

First, we acknowledge everyone's point of view then we cast doubt on explanations (stories) through stories from our own relationships, through humor, or through simply teaching clients that psychological explanations are unreliable and the jury is still out on the TRUTH about why people do the things they do.

Articulating and Channeling:
Putting Words in
Clients' Mouths

If we must have explanations about behavior, then we choose to create explanations that will facilitate change. When we supervise therapists we suggest that they make only diagnoses that will lead to something to do differently in the client's life. At a workshop in 1980, Pat heard Jay Haley tell the story of supervising a therapist who had diagnosed a child as "depressed." Haley said that he would never let that be the problem instead he would call the problem "school phobia," because that would lead to something to do. We do the same thing in marital therapy. For example, if a wife says that her husband came from a family that did not show affection and that is why he doesn't show affection, we might say, "So you think he may have the feelings you want him to have but simply needs some remedial training." We move the explanation, rather than dispute it. We are putting words in the client's mouth that can support change.

By putting words in the client's mouth, the therapist acts as a translator for the partners. With the couple mentioned earlier, Jan and Rob, we found that saying "You really found out how much you loved her when she suddenly left," expanded on Rob's comment that he would have been glad to change, had he known how much it was going to hurt to have her gone. The "love" comment was not what he said, but when we expanded his statement he adamantly said, "Yes!"

Putting words in the clients' mouths can add positive, productive statements and block critical, provoking, or blaming statements during the therapy session. For example, we might respond to a blaming statement by translating it quickly to a request for something different. Consider a statement such as, "How can we have time for communication?! You're always watching sports and waving me off with your hand when I want to talk." We would translate this into, "So you are asking for some special times to be set aside for the two of you to talk." Or, "So if he wants you to let him finish a game would you like for him not to use the waving-off hand gesture and commit to a later time he will talk?"

The shift we are making involves moving from repetitive blaming statements focused on the past to actions they would like to have happen in the future. Usually the couple is already spending quite a bit of time at home rehashing the past and trying to determine whose fault things were. We want to move as quickly as we can from that orientation to the possibilities for solutions in the present and the future.

Inclusion Language

When couples talk about their problems, they often use language that suggests that the barriers they face can't be overcome.

A couple came to see us after the discovery and ending of the husband's affair. The wife was devastated. She said, "I just can't imagine that I will ever be able to trust him again. How could we have a future?"

Pat said that she thought that trust was based on positive predictability over time. If her husband continued to be loving and faithful over months or years, trust could and would grow again. "For a while you may continue to be fearful and distrustful, and that's probably appropriate and protective. And while you're feeling fear and distrust, you can still be in this relationship."

The wife had been seeing distrust and the future of the relationship as incompatible. Pat's response was intended to help her include her feelings in the future of the relationship.

In another case, a couple came to see Pat on the verge of a divorce. When the wife was asked what she wanted out of therapy, she answered, "Freedom." Pat asked her what freedom might look like in the context of her marriage. After some discussion, she started to articulate what had at first seemed impossible, for her to do some of the things she wanted and still be married. The next task, of course, was arranging for this possibility to become a reality.

Points of Agreement and Common Goals

One of the stories couples get stuck on is that they have nothing in common. Often this will be after a long history of raising children together and having developed a life together. Focusing on the commonality of this history can sometimes be done with gentle humor. When they propose that they have nothing in common, we can say, "Of course there are the exceptions of Michael, Jennifer, and Molly [the children's names]." We would also focus on what activities they might develop together, perhaps things neither of them had done before.

It is often easy to generate common goals in the area of emotions. Most people want to be loved, and when they come to therapy both spouses often feel hurt.

Larry and Yvonne, mentioned above, were about to celebrate their second anniversary when they came in for counseling. Even though they had only been married a short time, they talked about not having much in common. They were very traditionally male and female. Larry worked out daily and loved sports, while Yvonne liked decorating and sewing. As the session progressed they both talked about wanting more from the relationship. We pointed out that they had one very significant thing in common: wanting to be treated with affection. When we asked them to get specific, they defined "affection" in very similar ways, so they discovered they had that in common as well.

We usually begin by getting mutual agreement on some vague concern or goal upon which the couple can agree. Translating the concerns of each partner to something specific, such as eliminating rude voice tones and words, can give them a common goal. The task then becomes to define the specific actions that will lead to accomplishing that common goal or to clarify what actions constitute the contents for the empty words they have agreed on (for example, "What does 'rude' look like or sound like?").

We have found that making statements that highlight mutuality and connection, such as, "It is clear that you have similar values about the kind of lifestyle you two want," can create the same positive expectations that a good report from a physician creates. A couple came to us telling of their previous experience in therapy. They had taken their son to a local psychologist. The psychologist saw the whole family once and the child once. In the third session the therapist said to the couple alone, "I don't want to drop a bombshell, but I just have the feeling that the two of you don't want to be together." We were totally appalled when we heard how this therapist's story was imposed on the clients and the discouragement that resulted. We consider this an iatrogenic (treatment-caused) marital problem. As therapists we sometimes forget that in defining our clients' world views we have similar influence as a medical doctor. Hope is often an essential ingredient for change. If a physician told you that you would never again be healthy, it would be difficult to feel great. If a marital therapist predicts doom and misery in a marriage, it will take a courageous couple to overcome those predictions. The couple who had seen the psychologist came to us for marital therapy. Because that marriage did have many strengths, in only three sessions they felt secure about staying together and cleared up their communication problems.

Look for similarities and point those out to the couple. It is particularly helpful if those similarities are behaviors, such as both liking to cuddle in front of the television, but if those similarities are in the more abstract realm of wanting a happy marriage, they can still provide a starting place. We have found that the more abstract we have to be with the couple to find mutually agreeable goals, the more likely it is that it will be a treatment challenge. If the only commonality you can identify at first is not wanting nuclear war, you know that you are probably going to see the couple more than two or three sessions.

Filtering out Blaming or Provoking Statements

Both of us are determined to prevent more damage from occurring to the marriage during *our* sessions with the couple. As soon as we hear anything that moves towards blame, we act to prevent it.

Translating blame to an action request takes most of the power out of the blaming statement.

Judy had been married before and had two nearly grown children. John had not been married but had adopted a child who was now grown with a family of his own. Judy had felt she had been treated rudely by John and his grown child and that she was not included in family plans. John protested, "Well, if she would just be nice to my son and his wife everything would be fine!" Rather than going along with those vague goals, we started negotiation about what "being nice" would look like and what actions John could take to create an atmosphere that would make Judy feel welcomed when she was around John and his son's family.

Couples tend to get into dueling blame battles: "If she would only . . . " and "If he would just. . . . " If they have children, you can remind them of the common dilemma of deciding who started it. The "she hit me first!" of little children is often countered with "but he was staring at me!" Usually the couple will admit that it is very hard to tell who did what first. Larry and Yvonne, mentioned earlier, admitted that they could not tell if Yvonne got sensitive because Larry acted indifferent or if Larry withdrew because Yvonne was so sensitive. The longer the marriage, the more impossible it is to say who started the difficulty. We say, "We can rarely determine who the culprit is for the difficulties that are happening now, so let's just focus on what actions might help you heal now." Bill has a favorite phrase: "No one is to blame and everyone is responsible." We sometimes write that on a sheet of paper for the couple to take home and post in a prominent place.

To prevent blame or to interrupt rude behavior, we will often simply say "Stop!" in the middle of a client's negative statement. We say something like, "What you are starting to say is what you have been saying at home that is not working for you. Let's find a way to say what you want to say that will not make your partner turn out to be the bad guy." This is accompanied by a hand gesture similar to a referee's "time out" signal or by our simply holding up our hands like a policeman stopping traffic either gesture emphasizes the stop message. If clients can learn to stop themselves in a session with our coaching, then they can usually translate those changes to their interactions at home.

Finally, as mentioned earlier, our plan is changing from blame (which is oriented towards the past) to the person's goal (which orients him or her to the future). Saying, "So you were hurt and you wished she had said . . . instead," takes much of the sting out of the blame. Instead of focusing on blame statements, we move to solutions.

Identifying Strengths: What's Worked?

It seems to us that, whatever peoples' experiences are at the moment, they are likely to feel that they have felt the same way for a long time, even if that has not been the case. If we feel happy, it seems that we have been happy for a long time. If we are in a depressed mood, we tend to look on the bad times of our history and feel that we have felt that way for a long time. We try to coax people out of global negative thinking about the marriage by asking about when things were better. This not only tends to move them from thinking that everything is negative to adopting a more positive view, but also helps us identify what has worked in the past.

Rae Ann and Jerry were busy with a large Mormon family. They were both active in their careers and

were swamped with church activities. They had left
their relationship on the back burner for a long time.
We asked, "When are the times that you have had
good conversations in the past?" They agreed that
they had the best talks riding in the car, particularly
on long car trips from Omaha to Salt Lake City to
attend the Temple. We suggested that they make a
point of driving out to the Temple in Salt Lake City a
little more often so that they could have time for
conversation, and that they use shorter car trips, such
as a trip to a neighboring town for apples in the fall,
to keep the good momentum going. They found these
suggestions very helpful and began to put their attention to noticing ways to have more conversation time
on a regular basis.

•   •   •   •   •   •

Karen and Earl felt that they were drifting apart.
Karen was consumed by a career that she did not like
but felt trapped in because the money was excellent.
Earl was an elementary teacher who found conversation very difficult. We asked them when had they
found it easiest to talk in the past. They agreed that
they had their best conversations while on walks. We
suggested that they walk at least twice before the next
session. They came back and reported that they had
been talking much more easily both on walks and at
home. They had decided their marriage was okay and
Karen decided to focus instead on her dissatisfaction
with her job.

In this process we looked for exceptions to the problem, for times when the difficulty was not a difficulty.
When we are looking for exceptions we sometimes ask

about an earlier, more loving time in the relationship. We might say, "When you first fell in love, what types of things were you doing that you are not doing now?" Often they will answer with a number of romantic things, but sometimes they will recall various entertainments. The solution may be to do some of those things that worked to make them fall in love. That will help revitalize the romantic part of their marriage.

Be careful to ask about actions rather than personalities or conditions when searching for what was good about their relationship in the past. Bill once made the mistake of asking a couple what had attracted them to each other in the first place and the woman replied, "I was impressed by his pickup truck. He doesn't have it anymore, and even if he did, I'm not impressed by that kind of stuff these days." Talk about a conversation stopper!

We sometimes ask if, in the interval since the clients made the telephone call to schedule the session, they have noticed things have been going better. When they answer positively or when anything is volunteered about things going better before the initial session, we highlight that and suggest that it is a good sign. We often notice that improvements begin as soon as everyone pays attention to what improves the relationship.

Chris and Tim were coming to therapy for the first time. Their complaints were needing to feel closer and to not argue about disciplining of the children. Chris mentioned that since she had called for the appointment Tim, who was not usually a "toucher," had been much more affectionate physically. Bill responded, "I would think that more touching might be one of the things that you were wanting when you wanted to feel closer. Has that helped?" Chris agreed that that was one of the things she had wanted and we pointed out that they already seemed to be moving in the right direction. We then talked about how to keep this trend towards more closeness going.

In this case we empowered the clients by pointing out to them that they had been making positive changes on their own. Sometimes all the therapist needs to do is remind the couple of the things that have worked in the past. With just a little push, the couple begins to move in the right direction. When we highlight partners' strengths and encourage them to use the skills they already have, changes sometimes come about rather quickly.

To locate strengths and resources that the couple has but has neglected, we ask about what was happening when things were better, we hold positive strength-oriented assumptions, and we ask for exceptions to the rule of the problem. Implicit in our questions and comments is an assumption that the couple has resources for change.

Metaphors for New Understandings

We have given several examples of telling stories from our own relationship to inspire couples. We also tell stories from our family's, other clients', and friends' relationships. Here is one of our favorites:

Pat's parents, Lofton and Jessie Hudson, were about to have their 50th anniversary. Pat was making party plans when Lofton, who is averse to public celebrations, said that he would make a point of being out of the country if such a party were held! Pat discussed this alone with Jessie who said, "I really don't mind as long as he gets me a dozen yellow roses." Pat

asked, "Have you told him?" Jessie said that she had
not. When Pat went home and told her children at
the dinner table about this, Pat's daughter, Angie,
said, "It sounds like Grandma is expecting Grandpa
to read her mind and it is pretty illegible!"

We use this story when the barrier to change is that
one of the partners is expecting the other to become the
Amazing Kreskin (a stage performer who "reads minds")
about what he wants. Humor helps the clients realize that
expecting accurate mind reading from a partner may not
be reasonable. We also say that you don't want to have to
tell your partner over and over again what you want, but
a training period might be warranted.

By the way, the rest of the story about Lofton and Jessie
is that Pat told Lofton what Jessie wanted, and Jessie got
her dozen yellow roses (triangulation and enmeshment
with a happy ending!).

Another story that helps to get people moving in the
right direction is about one of the couples we saw in treatment:

Dan and Jean had been married for 12 years. Dan was
very romantic and Jean was a well-organized, orderly
person. As an assignment we suggested that they tell
the other person in videotalk three things that he or
she could do that would be "love" for them over the
next week. Dan wanted her to plan a surprise picnic,
call him at work, and, in the middle of vacuuming,
stop and give him a hug. Jean wanted Dan to help
with the dishes, call and arrange that the wallpaper
get hung in the family room, and to clean his whiskers out of the sink after he shaved in the morning.
Our first task was to help Dan get over believing that
his definition of love was the only valid one. He fi-

nally accepted that his wife's "practical" things, as well as his "romantic" things, could be part of love. This assignment worked so well for them that they later told us that they made a habit of beginning each day by asking each other what they could do that would look like love for the other that day.

We usually tell couples this story right after they have selected things that they are going to do for each other to show love. Hopefully that inspires them to develop loving habits for the long-term benefits, as Dan and Jean did.

Sometimes we don't tell stories per se but still use metaphorical interventions. Included in this category are rituals and symbols (see Chapter 6 for a more detailed discussion of these) and analogies.

Bill was working with a couple in which physical violence had occurred. The physical violence stopped, but about eight months after the couple had stopped seeing Bill on a regular basis, the wife came back alone. She wanted to be able to better deal with his "moodiness." She said she had not brought her husband because she considered this to be her problem. When we unpacked the empty word "moodiness," it involved her husband's yelling at her and calling her nasty names. Bill suggested that perhaps this was something he could change, but she was discouraged and had decided that he was just that way and would never change. She had decided that she would just have to get used to it if she were to stay married.

Bill had heard that this woman was an excellent horse trainer. She made her living training race horses and had a good reputation in town. He asked her what she would do if she were brought a horse that was impossible to train and she immediately shot back, "There's no such thing as an impossible-to-train horse!" When Bill asked how she trained difficult horses, she told him that there were four simple principles of horse training. The first was to select a method of training that worked and that one was comfortable with and to use that consistently. The second principle was to only teach the horse one new thing in each training session, as trying to add more than that only washed out the learning. The third was to never get angry at the horse and blame him for not learning. If one did, one should stop the training session right away, as getting hooked in also washed out the effectiveness of the training. The last was that the trainer sometimes had to give up the little controls to stay in charge of the training. She explained that sometimes the horse would be fighting her and she would drop the reins. The horse would then stop fighting and she would gradually reestablish her control.

At the end of this little lesson, Bill told her she knew everything she needed to know about how to "train" her husband to stop being so moody and to speak respectfully to her. She brightened up and agreed.

This last case involved using an analogy, horse training, to help the woman find a view that would help her solve her marital problem. She was also reminded of a context in which she was competent and of skills she could transfer from one area to another (see O'Hanlon & Wilk, 1987; O'Hanlon & Weiner-Davis, 1988).

Changing the viewing and the doing can be fostered by task assignments, humor, pattern changes, rituals, and setting limits and consequences. These topics will be discussed in subsequent chapters.

4

CHANGING THE "DOING" OF THE COUPLE'S SITUATION

Pattern Intervention

There was once a man who set off in search of wisdom. He wanted to know how the world worked and what people were all about and the wisdom that had been gathered so far in the history of the world. He studied and practiced spiritual disciplines from all different cultures. He studied and practiced physical disciplines like sports and yoga. He studied and mastered many academic disciplines. He started with the "hard sciences" like physics, chemistry, geography, etc. Then he studied and mastered some of the "soft" sciences like economics, sociology, and anthropology.

Finally he came to psychology. By now he had gotten very good at sifting the wheat from the chaff in each discipline, so he wasted no time going to the heart of psychology. He knew that in the soft sciences there was a lot of speculation and he wanted only the aspects of psychology that had been proven to have empirical evidence behind them. He found a book in the library that he thought would be just the thing he needed. It was called *Things Psychology Has Proven*. (It was rather a slim volume.) Upon reading it, he found that what psychology has proven is mostly that rats can be put in labyrinths and can learn to negotiate those labyrinths and to remember what they have learned.

You know the typical rat lab experiment. The labyrinth is a maze of tunnels with many blind alleys and dead-ends. There are slots at the end of several tunnels that can be lifted up and down to make new exits from the maze. The experimenter places a hungry rat at the beginning of a maze and puts cheese at the end of a particular tunnel to find out how long it takes the rat to learn the maze. In a particular experiment, the experimenter may lift up the slot on the fourth tunnel and put cheese there. After many false starts and unsuccessful tries, the rat finally negotiates the maze and finds the cheese at the end of the fourth tunnel. The experimenter dutifully records how many trials it takes the rat to learn the maze. Once the rat learns the maze, the experimenter can show that the behavior that has been learned can be extinguished, or unlearned. Perhaps the experimenter puts the cheese at the end of the second tunnel this time and closes the slot at the end of the fourth tunnel. At first the rat will run down the fourth tunnel, sniff around for the cheese, retrace his steps and then head down the tunnel again. He does this for some time until he finally gets hungry enough to set off on other paths and eventually find the exit and the cheese down the second tunnel.

The man closed the book on psychology and decided that this really didn't help him much in his quest for wisdom. He had already gathered enough wisdom to know that these experiments showed that rats were smarter than human beings. Rats would eventually go and look for the cheese, but human

beings would go down that fourth tunnel again and
again looking for the cheese. They would tell themselves the story that the cheese had been down here
before so it must be down here now, that the cheese
had been down here in their parents' relationships so
it must be down here for them, that they had learned
in school that it was down here so they would just
hang around and wait for it to show up. In fact, some
of the humans might even set up lawn chairs at the
end of the fourth tunnel and wait for the cheese. Rats
only go for the cheese humans can eat their stories
for years and develop patterns that they continue
for decades, even when it doesn't give them any
cheese.

One of the major shifts that has come out of systems
theory is moving from seeing people as set in their ways to
seeing people as participating in patterns. We have already
discussed some of the language patterns, the patterns of
viewing and communicating, that people use. The process
of specifying individuals' vague, blaming, and invalidating
comments into action complaints, requests, and meaningful praise is part of changing those viewing patterns. Here
we take up changing the "doing" patterns.

Pattern Intervention:
The Butterfly Effect

We view what couples do with one another as changeable
patterns, not set conditions. A similar view was put forth
by meteorologist Edward Lorenz, who was using a computer to analyze the effects a small change would have on
global weather patterns. What he found was that the most
minute changes have a profound effect on complex systems like weather. This effect was dubbed the "butterfly
effect," because, as Lorenz put it, if a butterfly flapped its

wings in Brazil, it might produce a tornado in Texas. Lorenz found that when he had a computer graphically represent the patterns of what seemed random and chaotic, there were points of order—"strange attractors"—that organized the chaos into beautiful shapes and patterns (Gleick, 1987).

In therapy we seek to alter the "strange attractors" of relationship patterns by introducing change. We find the points of order in the seeming chaos of the client's presenting situation and systematically perturb those pattern organizers.

Couples get into habits and patterns that become like a dance. We try to help them find new steps to do for the dances in which they step on one another's feet. We don't have any particular explanation for how these dances came about or what holds them in place. These patterns are merely what people are doing with one another. We are much more interested in changing the dances the couples tell us they want to change than in discovering where they learned to dance.

Identifying and Changing Any Regularities

We seek to identify, in videotalk or by observation, any regularities in the patterns of interactions around the relationship problems the partners report. We are searching for anything that repeats again and again and is changeable by direct actions people can take. Out-of-session patterns we search for are regularities in time, place, body behavior (including gestures and facial expressions), voice tone, voice volume, voice pitch, modality of expression, words, or any other invariant part of the problem pattern. In-session patterns include all of the above except time and place interventions.

Pat was working with a situation in which the woman would regularly yell at her husband and say pretty terrible things to him, like, "I'd like to cut your balls off!" (We don't know about you, but we thought that this was pretty terrible.) When Pat talked to the man alone one time, she asked what he usually did while his wife was yelling at him. He said that he just stood silently. Pat suggested some new possibilities. He might stick his finger down his throat and vomit. This would be different, she said. However, he said it didn't appeal to him. Or he might hide under the table. He liked this one and followed through on it. It stopped his wife in her tracks. She stopped yelling and asked what he was doing. Pat also suggested that he get a water pistol and shoot it at his wife. When he did this one, his wife began to laugh and get playful with him, dropping the screaming and anger immediately. Pat suggested that he could announce that he was leaving for one hour. That interrupted the screaming. Pat wondered if he had ever told his wife that what she said hurt his feelings, as he had indicated when talking to Pat. In spite of enduring this for over 20 years, he had never said anything to his wife about the pain of hearing these things she yelled at him when she was upset. When he told his wife, that also made a difference in the pattern. When the husband returned for some vocational counseling a year later, he reported that the verbal attacks had stopped completely and that the spouses had become more of a team.

Changing patterns is called pattern intervention. The goal is to modify some part of a repetitive aspect of the couple's behavior by changing or adding something to the pattern. There are four aspects that we might change:

the performance, the setting, the sequence, or the interaction. In the above example the sequence and interaction were changed. In the following example, the performance is altered, which affected the sequence as well.

Bill worked with a couple in which the complaint was that the woman had premenstrual syndrome (PMS). The woman wanted to be hypnotized to get rid of the PMS symptoms. When Bill asked them what gave them the idea that she had PMS, they told horror stories about her premenstrual behavior. She would, by her own account, get a mean look on her face (she had looked in the mirror and her husband agreed) she would fly off the handle at her husband or kids without provocation she would even get violent (she had once ripped the phone out of the wall—it was the old type, designed to be permanent—and thrown it through a stereo speaker) and she felt tense and physically bad (she was currently on hormone treatment prescribed by her physician). The couple described how the family had divided into camps, mother vs. father and the kids, as he would protect the children from her raging mood swings.

With this background, Bill was quite surprised to find that the woman, who worked at a clothing store, reported that she did none of this behavior at work, although she did feel physically bad during her PMS times even at work. Bill said that he was unconvinced, therefore, that it was purely PMS. He asked the woman to keep a chart of the times when she did the "PMS" behavior for the next month. He also suggested that what had split the family into camps, in part, was that the kids and the husband never knew when she might erupt, as she did not have PMS during every menstrual cycle.

Noticing that she dressed very stylishly, Bill asked if she had any piece of clothing that she would feel silly wearing. She said that she had a pair of bunny pajamas with feet and tail that her husband had given her as a gag gift some years before but she had never worn. Perfect, Bill said. He suggested that when she had serious PMS feelings, as a signal to her husband and children, she should, immediately upon arriving home from work, before she said a word to anyone, go to her room and put on those bunny pajamas. She and her husband were amused at the thought of this.

When they returned a month later, she reported that she was now convinced that her behavior was only partially related to her PMS feelings, as it happened at various times in her cycle. New things had been happening in the family as well. When the woman emerged from her bedroom wearing the bunny pajamas, the kids and the husband would scatter, knowing that she might explode at any time. She didn't usually explode, though, because she felt so absurd wearing the pajamas that she found it hard to work up a rage.

We focus on changing the setting with a couple by finding out about where a problem pattern occurs and changing the location. For example, if we find out that the couple usually fights in the bedroom, we say that it is not the best idea to have that room associated with fighting, so how about fighting only in some other room, like the laundry room? One of our supervisees took this a step further.

One of Bill's supervisees told Bill that he had tried the idea of pattern intervention and found that it really worked. When Bill asked him what he had done, he replied that he had suggested to an argumentative couple that they move to the bathroom whenever a fight was starting. In the bathroom the husband was to sit on the toilet with his clothes off and the wife was to lie down in the tub with her clothes on. During the next fight, they were to switch places, with the husband clothed in the tub and the wife naked on the toilet. The couple had reported that whenever they tried this they would burst out laughing and the fight would be over. Bill was impressed by the supervisee's creativity.

Challenging Stereotypes

As we mentioned in earlier chapters, one of the main difficulties we see in relationships is the stereotyping of one or both partners in ways that blame them or close down the possibilities for change. "Stereotyping" is an interesting word, because the "stereo" part of the word implies that it takes two to make a stereotype (as in stereo, two channels, verses mono, one channel). What often happens is that one person characterizes the other and this leads to a self-fulfilling prophecy (or perhaps an other-fulfilling prophecy).

One of the pattern interventions we try to effect is to get the person who has the label to act in a way that challenges the label. This changes the actions and the viewing at the same time. Again, this reflects our view that these labels aren't indicative of set genetic or personality traits, but are actions and habits that can be changed.

A couple sought help from Pat. The wife decided to attend the first session alone, as she had some things she wanted to say before the spouses came in to-

gether. The husband called before that first session
to tell Pat that, whatever his wife said, he wanted to
save the marriage and was willing to do anything to
keep them together. When the woman came in for
the first session, she said that she had little hope for
the situation and wanted to let Pat know that before
she met with the two of them.

The problem was, she said, that her husband was a
wimp. When Pat asked for some examples, the
woman talked about many times when she would get
angry at her husband and he would do anything and
everything to try to calm her down and placate her
so she would not be angry at him anymore. She
would often get more angry at his attempts to placate,
leading him to more desperately try to please her.
She would come home from work after one of their
disagreements to find that he had cleaned the entire
house and had made her some special treat, usually a
dessert. Many woman would be pleased with this, she
knew, but for her it had become another sign of her
husband's inability to deal with her anger. He was
a wimp, born a wimp and would die a wimp, to
hear her tell it. He couldn't handle anger and could
not stand up to her. She was tired of this and wanted
out.

Pat knew that the husband, as desperate as he had
sounded in his earlier call to her, would probably be
calling after this initial session, so she asked the
woman if she had her permission to talk to the man
about what they had discussed in the session. The
woman assented. Not surprisingly, the man called
right after the session ended. Pat only had a few minutes before her next session, so she told the man that
his wife had him stereotyped as a wimp. He knew
that, he said, but what could he do to change it, he

wondered. Pat suggested that between then and the next session (two weeks away) he act in any way that would blow her image of him as a wimp.

At the next session, they arrived and told this story. One day they had been talking and things started to get heated. They tried to resolve things, but she had to leave for an evening shift at work. When she came home from work, they sat down to talk again and got into an argument. The husband held up his hand and told his wife to close her eyes, he had made her a surprise that was in the kitchen and he wanted to get it for her. She was frustrated. Here was the old pattern playing itself out again—he was trying to avoid her anger by placating. He insisted though and she dutifully closed her eyes. The next thing she knew he had thrown a banana cream pie in her face. At first she was shocked and angry, but in a minute she started to laugh in amusement and amazement that he could ever do such a thing. It was totally out of character. Of course, this was non-wimp behavior, but not exactly the type the woman wanted. It had served the purpose of showing that her husband was capable of acting differently, however.

Pat helped them negotiate some non-wimp actions that the woman wanted her husband to do. The main one that made a difference for her was to have him stand with his toes touching hers while they had an argument for 15 minutes. He did that and she rapidly became convinced that wimpness wasn't in his genes. This didn't solve all the problems in their relationship, but it went a long way towards convincing her that he was capable of changing and that it was worth her while to stick around and work on the marriage.

One Person Can
Make a Difference
in the Pattern

Following these ideas, it makes sense that one person can make changes in the relationship dance. It may take two to tango, but it's hard to tango if one person starts doing the fox-trot. Sometimes we only have access to one person in the relationship. The other refuses to attend sessions or is not available for one reason or another. We will deal with situations of extreme resistance and harmful and dangerous behavior in Chapter 8 here we are discussing situations that aren't quite so severe.

Again, the main point is to focus on who can effect change, rather than who is to blame or who caused the relationship problem. We think that either partner can effect changes in the pattern, regardless of how the problem came about.

How do we help clients do this? One method is to have them be our information gatherers, since we cannot directly observe the relationship patterns in our office. We help our clients use videotalk to describe for us the typical sequences and patterns around the problem. Then, with the clients, we collaboratively design some new actions and talk they can use with their partner that is likely to change the pattern.

We might have the person take some new actions that will break up the couple's stereotyped action patterns. The case above, in which Pat helped the man change his and his wife's pattern of her screaming terrible things at him is a good example of this.

Sometimes simply helping the person in our office to make specific complaints and requests rather than characterizing and blaming the partner brings about change. Or we might coach him or her to elicit from the partner more videotalk regarding the partner's complaints, requests, and praise.

Pat was having lunch with a woman friend who said that her husband said she was always bitching. Pat suggested that her friend ask the husband to teach her the difference between bitching and making a request. Her friend felt better right away because she knew her husband wanted to be a fair man and that this idea would work with him.

While we are supportive of even one partner's coming for therapy to change a two-person relationship, we have some suggestions for patterns that will encourage the missing partner to join us.

While we were eating dinner with friends we got into a discussion about what kind of therapy each of us had had in the past. It was clear that Pat felt more comfortable seeking therapy than Bill did. Someone asked Bill how he would feel if Pat sought therapy. He said he would be afraid that he would be made out to be the bad guy. Many people feel this way. We have heard numerous stories of relationships in which attending therapy aggravated the situation. Since we empathize with people who hesitate to come into therapy, we have developed three strategies to encourage a reluctant mate to come in for therapy: inspiration by the spouse in therapy, coaxing by the therapist, and fear.

Inspiration can come from the spouse in attendance making sure that the absent spouse knows that the motivation for seeking therapy is loving the absent spouse and being committed to making the relationship as good as possible for both of them. The therapist can make sure that the spouse who has come to therapy tells the other spouse that we understand that neither of them has felt loved for some time and that we are hoping to change that for both of them.

> Lyn and Scott had been married for eight years and had immersed themselves in their careers, postponing children. Lyn came to therapy alone. She said that she thought they should come together, but Scott thought they should be able to handle their own problems. Scott was an accountant and so we asked her to ask him if he thought people should be able to handle their own accounting problems. Since by her report they had neglected closeness, we strongly urged Lyn to do several of the intimate actions we had identified that very evening in order to let Scott know how much she loved him. Scott showed up for the next session.

By emphasizing positive, loving actions right away, instead of confrontive actions, the partner who is present may inspire the absent partner.

Direct coaxing by the therapist can also bring in a reluctant partner. Pat's father, Lofton, was particularly adept at this. With his gentle, commanding voice and a slight Southern accent, he would telephone the reluctant partner and say, "I need to get the full picture of what I am working with. I know there are two sides to every story and if I could see you, even for just one session, it would help me understand the situation. You do not have to talk about yourself if you don't choose to." This method worked well for him. We have occasionally done the same thing through a letter. Almost without exception, when reluctant spouses come in once and find they are not going to be blamed or invalidated, they are willing to return.

A third way to get a reluctant spouse into therapy is fear. This is not our favorite but it is often used without our intervention. When a spouse who is seeking therapy gets discouraged and chooses to move out or see an attorney for a fact-finding mission, the complacency of the missing spouse will often be swept away.

Whether or not the reluctant partner will come in for a session, we coach people to draw and hold clear limits on their partner's harmful or potentially harmful actions. Since this is dealt with extensively in Chapter 8, we will not go into detail about it here.

We have found pattern changes to be valuable in working with couples. We hope we model this for the couples we see. If videotalk doesn't work in therapy, we will focus on pattern intervention. If pattern intervention doesn't work, we will use inspiration. If inspiration doesn't work, we will suggest consequences that the spouses apply to themselves, and so forth. Changing patterns can help couples and can help therapists help couples.

5

TASK ASSIGNMENTS
Between-Session Change

Task assignments are crucial to the way we work in both individual and marital therapy. Ever since we began private practice we have felt that, when people spend their time and money to come in for a session, they deserve to have something to do differently when they walk out. We also think that therapy has been long on insight and understanding and a bit short on helping people take action to change their situations. Because of these views, we have both been adamant about giving task assignments to couples to carry out between sessions.

There are a few basic principles in constructing task assignments, as well as some task categories that will help you organize your thinking and planning of assignments.

68

General Guidelines for Making Task Assignments

In Chapter 3 on changing the viewing and Chapter 4 on changing the doing we discussed several possible task assignments. Some observations emerge from designing that kind of homework for the client.

Task assignments are opportunities to change something outside the therapy sessions right away. They create a map for making changes. For example, if a couple has not been spending enough time alone away from the children, suggesting that their bedroom be declared off limits for the children after 9:30 at night gives the couple an idea of how to create private time in the future.

Task Assignments are Co-created and Emerge from the Conversation

Therapists often ask how we get people to follow through with the assignments we give. Our first answer is that these tasks are not just the therapist's idea, but are decided upon collaboratively with the couple. While there are assignments that we frequently give, assignments emerge from the conversation with the couple, so they are tailored for that couple and co-created with the couple. For example, the assignment to tell each other three things to do that would show love for them this week is something that we assign frequently but not always. When spouses are separated, for instance, we might choose an assignment that would focus attention on what needs to happen for them to be living under the same roof.

These assignments follow the same principles we teach couples in therapy about being specific with each other.

Any request made as part of a task assignment has to be in
videotalk.

Linda and Ray had been separated for three months
when they came for therapy. They were in a second
marriage and during the last 12 years they had had
seven kids living with them, including the one child
they had in common. Raising the children had been
difficult, but now there were only two still living at
home. Linda gave three reasons for moving out: One,
she did not feel that she was a high priority for Ray;
two, she felt that Ray was financially too irresponsible with money; and three, she could not stand the
old beaten-up house that they had chosen to accom-
modate all those people under one roof. Ray had gotten into financial trouble in a couple of ways. He had
purchased a franchise business that did not pay off
and he was supporting his 43-year-old sister. Linda
liked the sister, but she wanted more limits put on
the amount of financial help Ray would give her.

The task assignments fell into two categories. First,
we negotiated and agreed to a specific business plan.
Ray was to sell a mobile home he had purchased for
an investment. He had already started working an
extra job to get out of debt and to do something about
the house by spring. His idea was to level the house
they had been living in and to build a new house on
that site. When he brought this up during a session,
Linda was delighted with his idea. Since that house-
raising would be sometime distant, we agreed first on
Ray's selling the trailer in the next two months. This
was doable and Ray got right to it.

The second set of assignments fell in the area of
doing things together. Most couples we know have
to work to find time together, but in the case of Ray

and Linda this was extreme. Linda worked in a university food service and began work by 5:30 a.m., while Ray worked during the weekdays from 3:00 p.m. to midnight in a large industrial plant and on the weekends from 2:00 a.m. to 10:00 a.m. as a night watchman. This did not leave many opportunities for time together. They agreed on breakfast twice a week. This plus a few telephone calls was all that could be worked into their schedule. In spite of these overwhelming time constraints, when she saw action from Ray indicating that their relationship was a priority, Linda started to feel that Ray loved her.

These tasks were challenging to negotiate because there were so many practical barriers that seemed impossible to surmount. However, the little openings that emerged did make a difference. Notice that the concepts of "being irresponsible" and "not caring about" got translated, albeit not easily, into the videotalk of selling the trailer and having breakfast. These were co-created by all of us together and negotiated before being finalized. It took a few months and many more assignments for this couple to get back under the same roof, but ultimately they stayed together and were happy they did.

We have lots of ideas for task assignments, but we often find that if we listen carefully to our clients, they give us the best ones. During a session with a couple, the woman was complaining that the man did not usually communicate his feelings. A portion of the session follows:

WIFE: You know, one of the big things that led to a lot of our troubles is that he wasn't telling me how he feels. A lot of times, like last weekend are very stressful. We moved into our apartment, we all were sick with colds and everything, and he just kind of phased out on me. He was just like kinda not there, and I said, "What's going on? How are you feeling? What are you doing?" "Okay, I'm alright, okay." And it's like, if it's just the stress of moving in together, just tell me what you're feeling and a lot of times he doesn't do that, he doesn't deal with that. . . .

HUSBAND: I'm usually the last to know how I feel!

BILL: (Laughs) It's like, "I wonder how I do feel." And so during those recent conversations that you've had, when you've been sitting down together every night, have you been able to say a little more about what you're feeling?

HUSBAND: Sometimes.

BILL: Sometimes. Okay, so it takes a little practice to tune in to what you are feeling.

HUSBAND: I need some kind of an exercise or something that would help me do that.

BILL: Okay.

HUSBAND: I could sit down and write. I'm able to do that much better than talking.

BILL: Good, okay. So how about keeping a journal in preparation for your nightly talks, sort of like Olympic trials? You write out what's going on with you or what's been going on with you in the last day or so. It's funny that you mentioned writing, because sometimes when I have couples that get into these real blocked or stuck places in communicating, I just tell 'em, "Okay, get a pad of paper. Now you write out what's going on with you or what you want to say and you've got five minutes to do it (you set the kitchen timer or you can time it on your watch) and then you pass the pad of paper to her and she'll write out what's going on with her and then you pass it back and forth." So sometimes because she's maybe a little better with expressing it in words and you may be a little better expressing in writing, you may want to switch back and forth between those . . .

WIFE: We kind of, we kind of did that, just to see if we were on the same wavelength, when we were getting back together. We sat down at one point, before he had moved back in, and we wrote down what our short-term goals were and our long-term goals, just to see if we were on the same wavelength.

This couple had fine ideas about what to do. The husband indicated that he needed an exercise to help him express his feelings. As Bill was trying to think of a clever idea, the husband gave him one—he could sit down and write his feelings, which he found much easier than talking about them. The wife then reported that they had already used this technique to get aligned on their goals. This kind of assignment is the best, since we already know the couple or the person has the capability and willingness to do it and to fit it into the demands of their daily life.

Invite Objections and Ask About Barriers

Another principle for creating task assignments is to invite objections. We often ask clients to tell us what might keep them from doing the assignment. For example, they might say that, if their child has a test in school the next day and needs help studying, then the 9:30 time for keeping the children out of the bedroom may be delayed. We can then make plans for such contingencies, such as agreeing that only half an hour will be devoted to the studying. Of course, asking at dinner, "Is there any homework that you need help with tonight?" is also an excellent strategy. Ask for barriers and objections and have those taken care of before the couple leaves to increase the likelihood that they will carry out the task.

Often, when we want to help partners start to reinstitute a nonexistent or troubled sexual relationship, we ask them to give each other body massages. When we ask about obstacles to following the assignment, they might say that they are concerned about privacy. We may learn that they have no lock on their bedroom door, so we have to deal with some very practical matters before we can expect them to follow through with the task.

As we move away from strictly massage touching, sometimes other barriers or concerns emerge. One is that, even if there are locks on the doors, one or both of the partners might feel inhibited by wondering if one of their children might hear their sexual noises. We discuss options to deal with this concern. One common solution is to have pleasant music playing just loud enough to mask noises. Another might be asking the children to give the parents some quiet time when they don't come near the bedroom.

Another common barrier is that one person says that he or she is just not feeling close enough to willingly do intimate sexual behaviors with the other. We acknowledge this by saying, "So you don't feel you're ready yet." (Notice the expectancy word *yet*.) We then discuss what it will take for the person to feel ready to engage in those intimate behaviors.

The Experiment Frame

When the relationship has been difficult for a long time, the spouses may be skeptical that anything is going to work to make the situation better. Many times they will say, "Nothing will help, we've tried everything!" We will frame the task, therefore, as an experiment to see how they might feel if they did even something they have done before. By emphasizing that this is not something that has to be done forever, but something that they are going to experiment with for two weeks, resistance to long-term commitment to repeat actions is countered.

We would typically encourage this experimental attitude by saying, "I wonder what would happen if you, just between now and the next session, experimented with. . . ." Here we are inviting, not demanding, which also models an openness for negotiation that we hope the spouses will use with each other. We add, "We can see how this works and then, when we get together next week, we can make any adjustments that might be needed."

Use Expectancy Language

Another method for encouraging compliance with the task assignment is to use language that suggests that the couple will comply. "*After* you do this, I want you to tell me exactly what happened when you did the task, as if you have seen it on a videotape." Or, "*When* you spend this daily time together away from the kids, I would like for you to keep track of how often you have sex compared to now." Language that presumes that the couple will complete the task tends to create an expectancy that makes it more likely that the task will be done (O'Hanlon, 1987; O'Hanlon & Weiner-Davis, 1989).

We have found that telling stories about others who have successfully resolved something by doing some task creates more compliance and expectancy for change. Often when we give the assignment to do three things that would equal love for each other, we tell a story about another couple who found the assignment so helpful that they continued for years to wake up and ask each other what they could do that would equal love.

Combining expectancy and metaphor, you might say something like, "After you spend this special time together, you may discover what it is like to be lovers again, something you have put aside to be parents.'' Sometimes new therapists or therapists awed by the idea of metaphors forget that some simple analogy can get the point across. Vast knowledge of Greek mythology is not essential to doing marital therapy.

Another way to get couples to follow through with assignments is to use humor. Pat sometimes says to couples who haven't followed through, "I wish I was rich enough to blow this kind of money on a therapy session and then ignore the advice.'' This kind of teasing can lighten up the session and make the very serious point that results are contingent upon the couple's own efforts.

Having detailed methods for engaging clients in performing tasks, we now consider the types of tasks we usually give in marital therapy: pattern intervention, skillbuilding, and perception-shifting tasks.

Types of Task Assignments

Pattern Intervention

Pattern intervention, the subject of Chapter 4, is crucial to what we do with couples. Couples usually fall into repetitive patterns. Most of the time these repeating patterns will support the relationship, such as routines for initiating sex, handling the daily tasks of family living, and resolving conflicts. Occasionally the couple will have gotten into a pattern that is not supporting the relationship that is when we use pattern intervention. We sometimes tell couples that the only difference between a rut and a grave is the dimensions.

In physiological psychology, there is a concept called "reverberating circuits," which refers to the tendency for a set of neurons to get into a pattern of repeating firings. It is almost as if there gets to be a groove in the brain. Couples seem to get into reverberating circuits in their marriages. Finding a way to interrupt that groove with either humor or simply some new reaction on one person's part can make a big difference.

Skill-Building Tasks

The most common complaint that marital therapists hear is, "We don't communicate." Building communications skills, conflict resolution skills, and negotiation skills is a part of marital therapy. Task assignments provide a way of getting specific with the partners about what they are to do to practice new skills. Skill-building tasks fall into two categories: (a) making a task assignment about the *process* of the skill to be built and (b) making assignments that are specific to the skill to be built.

An example of making an assignment about the process of the communication would be asking the spouses to transform their complaints into requests to do the opposite of the behavior they do not like.

Mike and Jill were in conflict over their teenage daughter, Lisa. Jill felt Mike was too lax and Mike felt Jill "raved" about what she wanted him to do about Lisa. We asked Mike to let Jill know when she was doing what he called "raving" and to offer her suggestions about what he would like for her to say instead.

Using feedback from both spouses, we told Jill, "The next time you feel upset with Mike for not telling Lisa what needs to be done before she leaves for a date, ask him to make a written list of the chores that must be completed to earn the right to go out on a date and to deliver it to Lisa. He can tell her then

that these things must be done before she leaves and
refuse to argue with her about it. Do all this without
labeling Mike." This assignment would bypass Jill's
urge to "rave."

Pat often writes on the task assignment sheet, "Make
requests in videotalk," and asks the couple to put that
sheet on the refrigerator. In general, she does more edu-
cating about the principles to improve the process, while
Bill typically gives more practice without much talk about
general principles. Either method can work.

Sometimes one of the partners lacks the motivation to
acquire or relearn the skill.

Larry and Yvonne (see pp. 39 and 42–43) had conflicts about the quantity and quality of their time together. Larry liked to work out and was a runner.
Yvonne felt that she was not given enough of his
time and that Larry was not romantic when they were
together. Larry wanted her to stop nagging him about
going to work out or to run. To increase both
spouses' motivation, we tied the task assignments
about time and permission to go exercise together.
Larry was to spend a half-hour a day talking to
Yvonne about her day and sharing his day, in exchange for her supporting his exercise regimen by
not complaining about his being gone, as long as his
exercise time did not exceed eight hours per week.

Tying the task assignments together, so that both feel
that they are doing something, has two advantages. Both
partners feel that you, as the therapist, are taking the time
to respond to their unmet needs and are not taking sides.
Also, it makes task completion more likely by stimulating

a little competitiveness. People rarely want to face the therapist the next session after not having done their half.

The more longstanding the difficulties, the smaller the steps needed to get back on the right track.

> Barb and Tom had been married for 16 years. For the last two years they had not had sex. Earlier in their marriage, they had enjoyed sex. However, fighting and lack of attention to the relationship had led to no physical contact for a long time. We gave a communication assignment about requests and complaints and an assignment to hold hands while watching television at night. We felt an assignment to have sex would have been ignored, but an assignment to hold hands, followed in the next session by an assignment to do back rubs, was a small step that would help them become comfortable with touch again.

Perception-Shifting Tasks

Tasks that are designed to get the partners to orient their attention either to an aspect of the difficulty they have not noticed before or to some aspect of their relationship they have not noticed before are called perception-shifting tasks.

> LeAnne and Carl had experienced violence in the past. Carl would get angrier and angrier and eventually he would hit LeAnne. Among the many things that we did with this couple was a task assignment involving the early warning signs of impending violence. We asked what the earliest sign was that things were going to get out of hand. LeAnne reported that Carl would sit on the sofa with his legs outstretched,

his arms folded across his chest and his lips clamped
shut. Carl had not noticed that before. They agreed
that the way to avoid the escalation was to have Carl
take a break and leave the house for an hour and cool
down.

For this couple, sensitivity to a perceptual cue that they
had not talked about before and an assignment related to
that helped stopped the violence cycle.

Another type of perception-shifting task is to ask the
spouses to try to catch each other doing something right
(O'Hanlon & Weiner-Davis, 1989). We sometimes ask
them to secretly make a list of the things the other person
did right and bring that secret list to the next session. This
gives an atmosphere of fun and playfulness. At times we
have combined this perceptual assignment with an assignment to do some special things for the partner and then
see if those things appear on the ''catch-them-doing-
something-right'' list when the couple returns for the next
session.

Another way that we can encourage perceptual change
is illustrated by a conversation Pat had with a friend about
the friend's husband.

Rachel, a therapist, was complaining that her husband would react to her requests as though her main
motive was to control him. He would usually raise
his voice and say, ''Don't tell me what to do!'' Pat
asked if he usually went ahead and did what she
asked even though he implied he was not going to.
Rachel was quiet for a moment while she reviewed
recent history in her mind. She was clearly relieved
when she realized that, in spite of his bluster, her
husband usually did do what she asked him to do.

Actions, not words, are usually more significant in a relationship.

Earlier we talked about seeing our task as therapists as helping to change the viewing and the doing of couples' problematic situations. Pattern intervention and skill-building tasks are used to change the doing of couples' difficulties. Perception-shifting tasks and therapeutic symbols and rituals (special types of task assignments we use so frequently that we have devoted the entire next chapter to them) are used to modify the viewing of the marital problems.

Whatever task assignment is used, we feel that it is part of providing quality service to give clients something that they can do at home. One of our colleagues mentioned that she has difficulty thinking of task ideas when the couple is there for the session. Since this particular therapist is good at writing letters, we suggested that she write couples letters containing their assignment after the session.

Of course, not every assignment you give is going to work. The partners will, however, be able to tell how committed you are to helping them because you have given them something concrete and specific to do, rather than just nodding sagely and offering a wise interpretation. Thinking their way out of marital difficulties may be impossible. Doing their way out of them is more likely to work.

Written assignments are more powerful than only spoken ones. We put the assignment in writing and give a copy to the couple. We have a form that looks like a prescription pad and makes an automatic carbon. Our prescribing an assignment on this pad usually leads to a joking question, "Where can I get that filled?" We answer, "At your local relationship." Besides helping the couple re-

Figure 1
The Hudson Center Task Assignment Prescription Sheet

The Hudson Center
  for Brief Therapy   **TASK**   11926 Arbor St.
  (402) 330-1144   **ASSIGNMENTS** Omaha, NE 68144

CLIENT: _____

_____   _____/____/_____

      THERAPIST   **DATE**

member what they are supposed to do, the copy in our
notes lets us know exactly what we decided upon as the
task, making follow-through more consistent and accurate. If you are seeing 20 or 30 couples a week, task assignment sheets are a must. A copy of the form we use at the
Hudson Center is reproduced in Figure 1.

6

UNFINISHED BUSINESS
Using Rituals and Symbols to Resolve Tragedies

There are two different types of rituals. First there are the daily or special activities that people regularly engage in, such as eating dinner together, reading the paper together on Sundays, or holiday celebrations. This type of ritual provides stability in the midst of the constantly changing nature of life. Mary Catherine Bateson (1989) has written, "Relationships need the continuity of repeated actions and familiar space almost as much as human beings need food and shelter . . . " (p. 126). The second type of ritual involves ceremonies that are set apart from everyday life and used to mark transitions. In our work with couples we use rituals in both ways: restoring regular rituals that couples have neglected and creating healing ceremonies to help them move on when they are stuck. We design therapeutic rituals for three functions: to facilitate a transition to establish boundaries or connections or to heal from some painful event in the past.

Types of Symbols

Usually when we design a therapeutic ritual we select or create something as a symbol, that is, an object that represents something else. It may represent something invisible, like emotions, situations or relationships, or something concrete, such as a person.

One couple was haunted by the ghost of the wife's deceased husband. She was constantly comparing the new husband with the old husband. We thought that the wife needed to do some grief work in order to put her former husband to rest. Pat had recently attended a workshop by Jeff Zeig, an Ericksonian therapist, who had suggested having a client carry a rock as a symbol of a difficulty and then asking the client to dispose of the rock as a ritual symbolizing letting go of the problem. The woman in Pat's case was very particular about her appearance, so Pat recommended that she go to a lapidary shop and select a particularly attractive rock to carry around, one that would properly represent her previous marriage. The ritual of letting go of the past by symbolically burying the rock was combined with some typical interventions: increasing effective communication, agreeing to drop the subject of the deceased husband, and carrying out task assignments to empower the husband as a stepfather and husband so he could have greater influence and inclusion in the family.

In helping clients select an appropriate symbol for a therapeutic ritual, we distinguish three types of symbols: linked objects, created objects, and icons.

Linked Objects

Linked objects are symbols that were physically associated with the person or situation that the client is trying to resolve. When we asked one woman what would be a good symbol of her estranged husband, she selected a golf hat he had favored. Other examples of physically associated symbols are pillows that the person had slept upon, articles of clothing, or jewelry. Sometimes the exact object is not available, so an identical object may be purchased.

One couple who came to us for therapy had been separated for a year because of an affair the husband had had with a neighbor. The husband had given his girlfriend a key chain as a gift, which he could not, now, retrieve. In order to ceremonially end this painful time, the husband purchased a clear plastic key chain that had the name of the other woman on it and gave it to his wife. She smashed it with a hammer and then drove over it with her car (thus giving thorough expression to her rage).

Created Symbols

Created symbols can be created specifically for the ritual or can be already in existence, e.g., poems, letters, pictures, sculptures of the situation or person, or anything else constructed by the client. One of our supervisees, Jan Jones, was working with a woman whose sexual relationship in her marriage was negatively affected by a childhood incest experience with her brother. Jan assigned the woman the task of making drawings of her feelings about those experiences. She created very interesting drawings, showing the pain she experienced as a tiny shrunken figure and her rage as a giant red monster bursting off the page. This illustrates the process of getting the client to

create a symbol. Once the symbol was created, we would
have the woman plan a ritual for symbolically leaving the
pain in the past.

If there have been long-term unresolved issues, a continuous letter (van der Hart, 1983) can be a particularly
useful symbol. By "continuous" we mean that the person
is to write a letter as a daily ritual. This project can last for a
week or a month or longer. The client's sense of what still
needs to be expressed determines whether days, weeks, or
months are necessary to complete the continuous letter.
We have often used this assignment to help people deal
with the loss of someone through divorce or death.

> Jane and Will had been married two years. This was
> a second marriage for both of them. Jane's divorce
> had been very bitter and they both agreed that her
> anger towards her former husband was affecting her
> in this marriage. We had her sit in front of a picture
> of her ex-husband and write to him for 30 minutes a
> day for as long as she needed in order to feel that her
> feelings of rage towards him were dissipated. After
> three weeks of writing, Jane felt better. Then we had
> Jane and Will create a ceremony during which they
> destroyed the letter and the picture as a symbol of
> excluding this old relationship from their marriage.
> They followed this with a celebration.

Icons

Often a picture of the person or event will be used as
the symbol of the damaged relationship. Anything that
physically resembles the person, e.g., a bust or a picture,
we refer to as an icon. If there has been a lover interfering
in a marriage, the picture of that lover can serve as the
symbol to be used in a ritual.

Usually, in selecting or creating a symbol, the client and the therapist collaborate about what symbol is most representative. If the therapist thinks that it could be of value to have the client carry the symbol around for a while, then the weight and size of the symbol are important considerations.

Types of Rituals

After a symbol is selected, we help clients design and carry out a therapeutic ritual. We divide the rituals into six categories: continuity, passage, inclusion/exclusion, leaving behind, cleansing, and celebration (Imber-Black et al., 1988).

Rituals of Continuity

Often couples have become so overly involved in either their children's lives or their own careers that the marital relationship has been sacrificed in the process.

One couple we worked with had five children, all involved in highly consuming activities such as paper routes, swim team, and gymnastics. Their "couple time" had become eroded by family activities. Both of them had become convinced that the partner did not have any interest in them. Prior to marital therapy, the wife had developed an alcohol problem, which was resolved by inpatient treatment, and the husband had immersed himself in his work. An important part of their healing was to arrange time for just the two of them. Specifically, they were to let the the children know that after 10:00 p.m. the parents' room was off limits. The couple was to turn off the TV at 10:00 p.m. and talk for half an hour. They also arranged to go out as a couple without the kids once a week.

This type of repetitious activity provides the continuity of a couple's and family's life. Pat was giving a speech about communication and mentioned the importance of time alone for couples. A woman from the audience came up to Pat afterwards and said, "My husband and I have been married for 25 years and have three children. Every Thursday night we have gone out alone for dinner without the children. We have a good marriage and Thursdays are the reason."

For a family or a couple to have a sense of stability, it is vital to have ritual times and activities that give a sense that people are connected to one another and that the relationships are in some way protected by this continuity.

The issue of time for the relationship is a concern for many of the couples we see. We often give them examples of our own rituals of continuity. One of our favorites is lying in bed discussing cases and our day's activities every evening. Another ritual occurs on a yearly and monthly basis. We were married on the 23rd of February, so we have two rituals of continuity around that. The first is to take the 23rd of each month off and spend it together. The second is to use a week's vacation in February to celebrate our anniversary. This luxury of time might not be available to most couples, but perhaps going out to eat alone once a month is an option.

The powerful impact of rituals of continuity was emphasized by some recent research with alcoholic families. Jane Jacobs and Steve Wolin of George Washington University (1989) found that whether or not a family developed an identity as an alcoholic family and whether or not the next generation had an alcoholic in it were related to how disrupted the family rituals, such as dinners, vacations, and holidays, were by the alcoholic member. When the rituals were kept intact, the family was less likely to continue the alcoholism in the next generation and was less likely to think of itself as an alcoholic family. Jacobs and Wolin's work focuses on rebuilding family rituals that have been disrupted or discontinued due to heavy drinking. Rituals seem to provide a kind of relationship glue to help couples and families to survive and stay together through difficult times.

Rites of Passage

A rite of passage helps people change roles. This may involve taking a new role or leaving behind an old one. When a couple has a first baby they move from the roles of being spouses to becoming parents. Our society has the ritual of Lamaze (childbirth) classes to integrate the father into the childbirth process, thereby facilitating the transition for both spouses. Some couples get stuck in unhelpful roles.

> One couple we saw was stuck in the roles of "fragile mental patient" and "protective spouse." The wife had had a "nervous breakdown" several years before. During this time she had taken an enormous number of medications. The wife felt that she had recovered and was no longer the fragile creature she had been when she went through that difficult time. The husband, however, never brought up controversial issues and would not argue with the wife because he was still afraid that conflict would precipitate a breakdown. The wife wanted her husband to treat her as a normal woman and argue with her at times.

Through discussions we found out that they had a medicine cabinet full of empty prescription bottles that were kept just in case any of her symptoms returned. As a ritual Bill asked the couple to write down the prescription information and put it in a safety deposit box in a bank (away from their daily life). Then they were to put all the empty bottles in a chest and bury the chest. The husband was then to pick an argument with the wife. Carrying out this rite of passage allowed the couple to change from the mental patient-protector roles to a relationship with more freedom to express emotions and resolve conflicts.

Rituals of Inclusion/Exclusion

In couples work it is often necessary to have a ritual to redefine boundaries around a relationship, to indicate who is and who is not included in the relationship and on which occasion. Engagement parties given by family members would be a ritual of inclusion, saying in essence, "Welcome to the family. We accept and approve." Not inviting someone to an event such as Christmas dinner can give a message about exclusion.

We felt that it was important in creating our stepfamily that the children be the primary people who "stood up for us" in our wedding. Each of the kids lit a candle to initiate the ceremony. By including the three children from Pat's first marriage, we made a clear statement that parenting together was a part of our commitment to each other and that we were creating a new family group.

Some rituals are used to clarify boundaries and exclude someone or something from the couple's relationship. We have suggested that couples exclude the "other woman" or "other man" after an affair is over by jointly writing the other person a letter telling him and her of the renewed commitment to the marriage and asking for no more contact.

Daily rituals of inclusion and exclusion become part of any family but may be more crucial in a stepfamily. Designing rituals for including new members into blended or stepfamilies can be an important component of building new relationships. As we shall discuss later, designing rituals for declaring and clarifying the boundaries around the marital relationship can be crucial to the survival of intimacy between parents or stepparents.

Rituals of Mourning/Leaving Behind

In long-term relationships there are transitions, changes, losses, and gains. Designing a ceremony to define these transitions more clearly and to designate an end to certain painful stages can be an important role of the therapist.

A woman came into therapy reporting difficulty with her five-year-old daughter. As she talked, it became clear that the difficulty had begun after the mother lost a child at birth two years before. She had been anesthetized during the birth process and had not seen the badly deformed child. Her husband had been present at the birth and had had an opportunity to see the baby and grieve. There had not been a funeral, so we suggested a ceremony. The father was a minister who had kept a journal of his feelings during the loss of this child and was eager to participate in the ritual. The couple bought a doll, kept it for a week, and then had a burial in the backyard. (The ritual did not include the five-year-old.) The ritual gave the

wife an opportunity to share her feelings of inade-
quacy as a woman for having had a child so badly
deformed. The husband, who had felt more complete
about the loss, read from his journal as part of the
ceremony. This ritual brought them closer together.
(This was one of several methods we used to facilitate
change in this family. We also normalized the inde-
pendence of the daughter, often using stories from
our own family, and encouraged the parents to pick
a few simple rules they were willing to enforce.)

We have found that unresolved and sustained grief
about something outside the marriage can be disruptive to
the marriage. The death of a parent often interferes with a
marriage in two ways. The first is that the grieving spouse
may be absorbed with grief and inaccessible to his or her
spouse. More commonly, the loss may interfere with the
marriage because the grieving spouse may be disappointed
at the other's lack of support. A ceremony designed in
therapy can often help by giving the non-grieving spouse
a way to participate, even if the only thing he or she does
is protect the spouse from interference by the children
during the process. For the grieving spouse the ceremony
provides a way to facilitate the healing process.

Steve and Ellen came to therapy for what could only
be called standard marital therapy: communication
difficulties, disagreements over raising the children,
need for more closeness. Steve had mentioned in
passing his annoyance that Ellen refused to throw
away any of her deceased mother's things, even
though it had been years since the mother's death.
After the couple's conflicts were resolved, Ellen
asked for a session alone. She reported that her

mother had died three years before but that she still felt that her mother was watching and judging everything that she did. We asked Ellen to bring in three of her mother's less expensive possessions. She brought in a kitchen utensil, an iron, and a box of saving stamps from a now defunct company. We assigned her the task of carrying around the box of stamps for a week, telling her to keep it with her every minute. Even if she went to the bathroom in the middle of the night she was to carry the box with her. At the end of the week, she was to dispose of the box. Pat saw Ellen several months later at a shopping center and asked her about the assignment. She reported that she had thought it was silly, but that she had done the assignment, ultimately sending the box to be put in the basement of her mother's house in Wyoming, which Ellen owned for rental property income. After she had sent it off, she no longer felt that her mother was watching her. To the delight of her husband, she had finally gotten around to getting rid of most of her mother's things.

Leaving a painful event behind can be crucial to progress in the relationship. Designing a ritual to symbolize the end of events—e.g., reconciliation after an affair, the end of drinking as a problem, the end of any interference to a relationship—can help a couple move on in the relationship. It is important to be sure that enough talking, living, or forgiving has occurred before the ritual takes place. If you have a couple go through a ceremony for an affair before they feel they have settled the issues, then the ceremony will not accomplish a sense of ending. If it is too far past the appropriate time, then it will have little meaning for the clients. If there has been an affair, we will mention in the first session that it might be helpful for them to have a ceremony when they are ready for this to be completely over. This prepares them and gives them hope that it is possible for there to be an end to this painful time.

Sharon and Rod were both career officers in the military. They had been separated for a year, during which time Sharon had told Rod that she wanted a divorce and then, because Rod did not want a divorce, she had come to therapy to look at the possibility of salvaging the marriage. Sharon had felt unsupported in the marriage and had had repeated affairs. Rod had been faithful but was not good at closeness and support. Through therapy Sharon decided that she would work on the marriage again. They were reunited. During the time we were working on the relationship, Sharon found out that, when Rod had thought that the marriage was over, he had had a short affair with a married woman. Since they had both violated the marriage, they burned letters from the married woman and some things from Sharon's past and recommited to their marital vows. This ritual was followed by a champagne celebration and making love. Sharon and Rod told us that they could never have experienced the much needed intimacy without having admitted their infidelity. They felt close to each other for the first time in their marriage.

Sometimes the marriage is so bad that holding a ceremony for the death of that marriage can mark a new beginning. If the couple has had a long history of painful interactions and seems ready to commit to some new behaviors, then having a funeral for the old marriage can be the beginning of a new life.

Reversal Rituals

When couples have become stereotyped and rigid in their roles, we may prescribe a role reversal ritual.

> A couple came for therapy in regard to disagreements they had over managing their 14-year-old adopted daughter. This had led to marital problems. The husband, Jim, a behaviorist who specialized in children's problems in his professional work, had designed a program to bring the daughter in line. His wife, Jenny, was left at home to carry out the behavioral program that Jim had designed for the daughter, while he worked long hours away from home. Jenny was a "softy," by her own admission, and would often fail to enforce the program. Jim would come home, find that his program had not been followed, and then severely discipline the child, inventing new restrictions and consequences for the program. We arranged for them to have one week in which Jenny would design her own program, one that she felt comfortable with, for managing the daughter. Jim was to play a new role that week, that of nurturer to his daughter. He was supposed to be especially supportive and listen sympathetically to her (as Jenny usually had in the past). Much to Jim's surprise, the daughter's behavior improved, as did the couple's relationship.

Occasionally, we arrange for these role reversals to change every other day or every other week.

> One couple was in a constant struggle over frequency of sex. When they were first together, they had had intercourse four times per day. As the years went

on, however, the wife had grown less interested in sex as she became busier in her career. In response to this, the husband had grown more insistent about having sex. They had developed a pattern in which he would hint, blatantly or subtly, that he wanted to have sex and she would do all she could to avoid being in a situation in which he could give her those hints. She felt guilty and pressured all the time, she said. He felt guilty, needy, rejected and deprived all the time, he said. We arranged for one week to be her week, in which she was the only one who could initiate sexual interactions. The next week would be his week, in which he could initiate sexual interactions. They did this for one month, and he discovered that during her weeks they had sex much more frequently. When the pressure was off, she reported that she felt a lot more spontaneously sexual than when he pressured her. We mutually decided that every week from then on would be "her week."

Preparing for and Carrying out Rituals

Introducing/Co-Creating

The first step in preparing and carrying out rituals is to introduce the idea to the clients. Clients, when given some general ideas about rituals, can then become co-designers of the rituals. They are much more likely to carry out the rituals if they had a hand in designing them. Moreover, the rituals are much more likely to include meaningful elements if the clients help design them.

Preparation

Next is the preparation phase. Clients gather or create any symbols that are needed for the ceremony and also choose the time, place, and other elements of the ritual. As we mentioned earlier, it is important to ensure that clients do not perform the ritual until the time is right. "We will serve no ritual before its time," is our motto.

Performance

When the time is right and all the elements are in place, the couple or individual does the ritual. Sometimes it can be done in the therapist's office, but most often it is done elsewhere. Sometimes couples or individuals want us to attend their rituals outside the office, and if we consider it helpful, we do.

Cleansing/Bathing

We usually include cleansing or bathing as part of rituals, particularly rituals for leaving something in the past. Our usual recommendation is that a couple have a ritual bath. (In case you were wondering, we don't attend this part of the ritual.) We suggest that they light candles in the bathroom and have a special bath together. "Special" could mean a bubble bath or bath oil, clean towels, and bathing each other to symbolize helping each other wash away the painful era in their relationship.

> Sara and Eric had not been married very long. It was a second marriage and Eric had not "married in his heart," as he later put it. Eric had fallen in love with, though not had sex with, someone else, a relationship

he later saw as stupid. Sara was crushed by this and, given the short-term of their marriage, she was very hesitant to remain in the marriage. The therapy initially dealt with whether Eric was going to stay. Once it was clear to Eric that he wanted to be in a relationship with Sara for life and they had discussed the infatuation, they burned a picture of the other woman and her letters attempting to seduce Eric. Then they bathed each other and repeated their marriage vows. We had a chance to talk to them years later. They said that it might have been better to wait a couple of more months, because Sara was still too hurt and negative, but that it was an important symbol for them of the *beginning* of healing rather than the end of the event.

Celebration/Social Recognition

Over the years of using rituals we have come more frequently to include both cleansing and celebration in all the rituals that we design with clients. Just having a couple get rid of something is not enough. There needs to be a part of the ritual that makes a statement about returning to life without the difficulty.

Pat had a private ceremony for the end of her first marriage. She made a photocopy of her marriage license and divided the copy into sixteen little rectangles, each representing a year of the marriage. On her fireplace hearth, she arranged the rectangles in groups to represent the years in different locations: two in Lawrence, Kansas; three in Madison, Wisconsin; seven in Omaha, Nebraska; one in Washington, D.C.; and the rest back in Omaha. She lit candles and spent time remembering each year one by one. She then burned the rectangle that represented that year. This was followed by a time of prayer and asking

God for forgiveness for not being able to keep her vow of remaining in the marriage until death. That evening we went to one of the best restaurants in Omaha to celebrate our new beginning. This felt almost more significant than going to court, which had seemed like a shallow and insignificant event. Five minutes of uncontested legal business had not felt like the proper ending to a 16-year marriage. This ritual had the desired effect of facilitating a sense of completion. This is not to say that Pat never felt sad about the divorce after that, but the ending felt much more final to her.

Celebration is one way to get social recognition and acknowledgment of new roles, new feelings, and new relationships. In 12-step programs, there are celebrations marking a person's sobriety at regular intervals, first months, then years. This helps reinforce the new role of the person as sober. After significant others participate in celebrations, social interactions with them help keep the new roles and sense of the changes in place.

In the table that follows we have summarized the pertinent points in using rituals and symbols for healing in therapy.

Rituals and Symbols: The Meeting of Meanings, Feelings, and Actions

Using therapeutic symbols and rituals is one way to bridge the gap between internal meanings, experience, and feelings and external actions. They are designed to externalize people's problems and give them something active to do in order to change their feelings or resolve the problem. Rituals and symbols serve, then, as special forms of task assignments that change both the viewing and the doing of couples' problems.

THERAPEUTICS SYMBOLS/RITUALS

Symbols

*Concrete objects that are connected with (*linked symbols*) or represent some situation, experience or person (*icons/created symbols*)
*Used to externalize an internal experience

Rituals

Regularly repeated activities
  Daily; seasonal; holidays
  Activities you can count on; stability

Rituals of Continuity
  Restoring previous rituals
  Prescribing a ritual that restores or makes connections to people or situations

or

Special activities marked out from everyday life
  Special time(s), place(s), clothing, foods, scents, activities
  Restricted to special people

Rites of Passage
  Designed to move people from one role or developmental phase to another and to have that validated and recognized by others in their social context

Rites of Inclusion/Exclusion
  Designed to make people part of or eject or bar people from a social group or relationship

(continued)

THERAPEUTICS SYMBOLS/RITUALS
(continued)

Rites of Mourning/Leaving Behind
Designed to facilitate or make concrete the end of some relationship or connection

Reversal Rituals
Designed to reverse roles in relationships or families

Phases
1. Introduction/co-creation; 2. Preparation; 3. Performance; 4. Cleansing/bathing; 5. Integration/celebration

When to Use
1. Unfinished business; 2. Stuck in some developmental phase; 3. To enhance separation (splitting) or connection (linking)

7

DEGRIMMING
Humor in Couples Therapy

Humor is an essential part of our therapy. Our fellow therapists at the Hudson Center have often commented on hearing laughter coming from our offices when we are in session. Humor is a natural part of what we do. Conceptually we see it as serving two purposes.

The first is to get the couple to be less grim about the situation in the session itself. The presence of humor in a session implies hopefulness. If the situation is too grim to allow any humor, then it is grim indeed. At the same time we are careful not to communicate that we see the couple's problems as trivial or frivolous.

The second purpose of using humor during the session is to either model a certain lightheartedness or remind the couple to use humor with each other outside the session. In our own relationship we have found that, when we seem to be headed towards an unproductive conflict, if one of us says something funny, we can avoid an escalation. Our five-year-old even uses this technique to sidetrack us from being upset with him. We help couples head off difficulties in the same way.

Is humor always appropriate? No, it has to be timed and used very carefully—with care and in a way that is full of caring. Some years ago, we sponsored a workshop by a therapist who uses teasing humor with clients. One of Pat's couples agreed to be a demonstration couple for the workshop. The husband was quite irritated by the excessive use of humor and refused to come back to therapy for two years! Pat's father used to say to frustrated parents, "You can teach knowledge but you can't teach wisdom. Experience will do that." We are counting on the couples we use humor with, as well as on the therapists we supervise, to attend carefully to when it is appropriate to be funny and when it is not.

One of the guidelines we have for using humor is that it should not be used in a way that blames or invalidates one or both of the partners. As Bill often says to Pat, "Remember, I'm not laughing with you, I'm laughing *at* you." (Just kidding!)

Jumping to Conclusions

Exaggeration of a situation or the outcome of a situation can be funny.

Leonard and Marge had had severe financial difficulties and disagreements over standards of cleanliness. Marge had been through two surgeries in the last year and that had contributed to her frustration with him and his frustration about money. She complained that Leonard would leave his clothes in the bathroom until the pile reached a height of two or three feet!

We began to tease Leonard by saying, "My gosh,
Leonard! What if she tripped over that mountain of
clothes! With her luck she would probably break
a hip and have to have a replacement. Then she
couldn't work for a few months. The house would
be repossessed. And all because you won't pick up
your clothes!" Leonard lightened up and then we explored what would get him to put his clothes in the
hamper. We hoped that the humor itself might be
one of the things that would remind Leonard to keep
his clothes picked up.

When one partner is discouraged and the other is looking for resources, we sometimes tell a story about Bill's
teasing Pat out of a blue day. Several years ago, before we
were married, Pat was feeling discouraged about life in
general and made a comment such as "Life sucks!" Bill
began to tease her: "Especially for you! You make more
money than 94% of the women your age. You have three
beautiful, intelligent children. You have a job that most
people would love, where you set your own hours. You
have parents who adore you and a man who is crazy about
you." Pat interrupted, "Okay! Maybe life doesn't suck!"
We both had a good laugh.

Pat has been known to borrow from her psychology
background for humor, particularly if the couple is familiar with educational psychology terminology.

Liz was a teacher who was married to an accountant,
Jeremy. From a previous session the assignment had
been, among other things, for Jeremy to hug Liz at
least once a day. When Pat asked about this, as they
reviewed the assignments and how things had gone,
Liz said, "He did hug, but he didn't do it right." Pat,

immediately seeing a chance for fun and change, said, "Are you telling me Jeremy needs some remedial hug training?! Both of you stand up and let's get right to it." We discovered that Jeremy's hugs had been too brief and that his hands were not placed firmly on Liz's back. So we agreed that he would remain in a hug for at least one minute (he could peek at his watch) and that he would firmly (but not so firmly as to block respiration) place both his hands on Liz's back. This lightened both of them up and also provided a lesson for them on getting specific, even if it was exaggerated for the moment.

Humor is a great way of teaching and shifting the context from one of tension and conflict to one of playfulness.

Candy had just related that her husband had had an affair the year before and that after she found out about it she had trouble sleeping and eating. A portion of the interview follows:

CANDY: At this point I could hardly sleep at all.

BILL: Because of the emotional upset and all that.

CANDY: So, um, but I have lost 59 pounds (*laughs*) since March.

BILL: So, is that good or is that bad?

CANDY: One good thing is that I have my figure back after having had a baby.

BILL: Maybe you can write a new diet book, *The Husband-Has-An-Affair Diet Book*. Maybe it's not for everybody, but I think there might be some money in it . . .

CANDY: (*Laughs*) Maybe.

Exaggerations of
Speech and Actions

We had a situation in our own relationship that changed the meaning of the word "acknowledge" forever. We have one thing that we argue about on a regular basis: who does what around the house. It may take us a lifetime to work this out. We were doing our usual listing to each other of all the things we each had done. Bill said, "I just want you to acknowledge that I do do some things around here." Pat went on talking about how unfair the task division was. Again Bill asked for acknowledgment. Pat continued to recite the history of the division of tasks and Bill asked a third time, "I just want you to acknowledge that I do do some of the work around here!" Pat responded by saying, "Okay! I [here you must thrust out your tongue in the middle of the word] acknahahahahaledge!" Both of us started laughing and the discussion finally moved on.

The situation can be exaggerated to provide humor, or the speech itself can provide the humor. Humor is not magic. It is something you can learn and that you can teach to your clients either directly or through modeling.

Puns

Puns are rampant at our dinner table and we use them in sessions too.

Bill was working with a woman who had been going with a man who was determined not to have an exclusive sexual relationship with her. She was discussing her difficulty in getting him to use a condom. She was debating whether or not to continue the relationship, but while she was deciding she wanted to avoid disease. She would discuss wearing a condom with her partner, but he would never end up wearing one. She tried leaving one discreetly on the nightstand next to the bed. This subtle attempt failed.

Bill had recently been at a conference where a family planning clinic had handed out a button that said, "Men—Wear a condom or beat it!" Bill gave her a button. She put it on with amusement and got the double meaning. We're still waiting to hear whether he put it on or not.

• • • • • •

A husband in a couple was reacting to his wife's ranting of the night before. "You need to be in an institution," he said. Before the wife had a chance to react, Bill interjected, "She already is—it's called marriage. And I'm going to see if I can get you both committed. One of the ways to be committed is not to undercut the other person's sense of herself, so I'd like you to find another way of telling her what you didn't like about what she did and we'll try to arrange for something different to happen in future discussions."

Stories and Jokes

We have already told many of our best therapeutic stories in this book. The story of the man whose wife thought he was a wimp, a stereotype he challenged with a banana cream pie, is a favorite. We tell this story to help one of the partners come up with something creative to do in the relationship to break the other spouse's characterizations.

The man in the couple Bill was seeing was harping on things that had happened many years ago. Bill asked him if he was Irish. The man said that he

wasn't. Bill was skeptical, but the man insisted he had
no Irish ancestors. Bill said that they had recently
discovered a new form of Alzheimer's: Irish Alzheimer's. It's a condition in which, as you grow
older, you forget everything but your grudges. He
was convinced the man was Irish, because he ap-
peared to have a rather severe case of Irish Alzheimer's coming on.

Shock and Surprise

We have mentioned before the idea of doing something
that breaks the spouses' rigid views of one another, as the
banana cream pie man did with his wife.

Rita and Nat had been married for 17 years and had
three children. Nat was a businessman who had gotten himself in a financial hole and had been working
more and more frantically. Their relationship had suf-
fered as Rita became more and more resentful. Finally, in classic mid-life-crisis style, Nat had, without
warning, walked out and started living with another
woman. Rita came alone to see us. She was eager to
save the marriage and ready to forgive the affair because she felt that she had driven him to it by neglect.
   The main complaint that Nat had had in the past
had been that Rita was a prude and not sexy. We
talked to her about doing something that would
shock Nat into the realization that she could change
and be sexy. Rita was very attractive, a tall, dark,
slender woman who dressed with elegant simplicity.
She decided to buy some sexy underwear, garterbelt,
and dark hose. We suggested that she put these on,
cover herself with a raincoat, go to Nat's office, walk
in, flash him, and say, "Look what you will be miss-

ing!'' She did this in a hit-and-run fashion to add to the shock effect and avoid rejection.

Another of our favorite stories is about a couple Pat was seeing that found an unusual way to intervene in a pattern.

Rose and Alex had both been married before. They were in an empty nest phase, where they had shifted from doting on children to doting on their dog. Rose complained that Alex paid more attention to the dog than he paid to her. Pat said, ''Well, why don't you both try acting like the dog? When Alex comes in the house, the dog doesn't sit in the other room waiting for Alex to seek him out. When Rose is watching television, the dog doesn't sit in the other room wondering when Rose is going to stop and pay attention to him. When Alex is reading the paper, the dog doesn't just wish that Alex would respond. The dog takes action!'' They were a little shocked and amused by this idea that the dog should be their coach. They agreed to observe the dog's behavior and imitate it between then and the next session. In doing so they broke the stand-off pattern they shared with many other individuals, that of waiting until the other person changes before they make any changes.

Amusing Confessions

Most therapists know that rapport–building can occur with a client if the therapist confesses that he or she once had a similar problem. Using humor can add to the normalizing and rapport-building that occur during therapy. When a woman complains that her spouse has not had sex with her in a year, Pat jokes that after five days she would get out the names and numbers of her favorite divorce attorneys! By exaggerating, we convey the message that it is acceptable to us that the person is upset at the same time we help the client not feel so grim about the situation.

We have found humor to be an essential part of our marriage and an essential part of our therapy. We trust you will use whatever humor you feel is appropriate. You don't have to be a stand-up comic to lighten up the situation. Even a little humor can create a context for change.

8

BOUNDARIES, ACCOUNTABILITY, AND CONSEQUENCES
Dealing With Destructive Behavior

When you are a marital therapist, you are bound to work with couples where one partner's behavior is far beyond the limit of acceptable adult behavior. This usually includes actions that are potentially or actually harmful physically, economically, or relationally.

One of our supervisees asked us how we decide which problem to deal with first when couples present multiple problems in marital therapy. We replied that we first take up the problems that are the most potentially destructive to the marriage or to either individual. Many of the problems dealt with in this chapter fall into those categories.

Soap Operas

We think of these unacceptable behaviors as soap opera behaviors, those things that you see in soap operas that turn them into drama. We are not saying that clients' motives are to create excitement. However, excitement and drama are what they get. We work with them to get them out of their soap operas.

The following is a partial list of soap opera behaviors: physical violence, excessive use of drugs and alcohol, lying, criminal behavior, gambling or sneaking money, jealousy, etc. When we see one of the partners because the other partner is doing one or many of these kinds of things, we anticipate a therapeutic challenge. On occasion, keeping the marriage going is no longer possible. We have a hierarchy of possible interventions that we use in our soap opera cases.

Making Sure Requests
Are Clear

We have presented our model for making positive complaints (objectively reporting the behavior that has occurred) and action requests (describing what behaviors the client wishes to occur). On our first level we will make sure that the partner who has been doing the excessive and inappropriate behaviors knows beyond a shadow of a doubt that there is a problem and it is serious.

> Robert and Lillian were a couple in their sixties. Since their last child left home, Robert had begun to drink alcohol excessively and would drink himself to sleep most evenings. Lillian was at her wits' end and sought therapy to see what she might do to keep him from dying of alcohol abuse. We found Robert to be some-

what embarrassed about the fact that his difficulty had reached this proportion. He readily agreed never to drink again. He also promised that, if he did not stop drinking completely, he would go to an inpatient chemical dependency treatment center. He set his own limit of total abstinence. In a follow-up interview over the phone two years later, we learned that Robert had maintained his sobriety.

Robert was unusually cooperative. Some might see it as a flight into health. If this was a flight into health, then it is fine with us as long as the flight was nonstop!

One way to look at the case of Robert and Lillian is to say that if you want someone to stop doing something, get his attention and ask him to stop. This seems obvious. However, sometimes we as therapists have developed such a complex view of why people are doing what they are doing that we forget to do the obvious and ask them to quit it! We also know that such cooperation and rapid change are theoretically impossible according to most contemporary theories of addiction. But apparently some of our clients are unfamiliar with these theories.

Of course, many situations are not quite so easy or straightforward to resolve. Our next level of intervention, then, is to identify and change the patterns involved in and surrounding the soap opera problems.

Changing Patterns

As we pointed out in Chapter 4, couples get into repetitive patterns around their problems, including out-of-control behavior. A pattern we have seen repeatedly with alcohol abuse is for the sober spouse to berate the drunken spouse.

Marge and Vic had a good relationship most of the time, except when they went to parties, which happened about once a month. The pattern was simple. Vic would become drunk and obnoxious towards Marge and others at the party. When it was time to leave, he would argue with Marge about who was going to drive home. After they did get home Marge would spend about an hour telling Vic what a bad, immature human being he was. The atmosphere in the home would be negative for a few days. Vic felt that his drinking was not a serious problem because he went for days without drinking and only "let loose" at parties. He felt that he had the right to do this. He admitted that he got a little out of hand, but felt that Marge was making a federal case out of nearly nothing. Her father had been an alcoholic and she, Vic felt, overreacted.

First, we got an agreement from Vic that he would let Marge drive home from parties. Second, we pointed out to Marge that in all the years she had been lecturing him about how disgusting and obnoxious he was for getting drunk, it had never moved him. We suggested that if she was upset after the party, she should stay up and write him a letter about what he was like at the party. The next day, after she had had a chance to think about what she had written, she was to decide whether what she had written was helpful or not. If she thought it might move him at all, then she was to give him the letter. Vic's drinking did decrease somewhat and the destructive and useless patterns around the post-party experience stopped.

Changing the pattern, then, is the second step in the escalating hierarchy of responses to inappropriate and dangerous behaviors. The third step is to make the boundaries or limits crystal clear.

Setting the Boundaries and Limits

When one person consistently acts in a destructive or dangerous manner, we help the partner or the couple define the limits and boundaries of acceptable behavior. We ensure that the boundary is defined in videotalk, so that both partners know when it has been breached.

> Rick and Emily had been married for four years. They had a one-year-old son, Michael. Since Michael's birth, the tension had increased between the parents. Rick had always been a serious party animal. He enjoyed drinking and gambling and hanging out with the guys. This had not been too much of a problem for Emily before they were married or even after they were married, until Michael came along. The behaviors that seemed acceptable to her as a husband were outside the realm of acceptability as a father of her son. She was particularly upset about the gambling, because the house payment had recently been late due to Rick's gambling losses.
>
> We negotiated an agreement about what the limits would be. Rick made a lot of money and felt that he should be allowed to gamble with it if that was his way of having fun. Emily agreed but wanted a cap on the amount Rick spent on gambling. They agreed that $400 a month was a reasonable amount. We suggested that this be kept in a separate account in which earnings and losses could be documented by bank records. Emily had access to this information at all

times so that she could monitor whether or not Rick
kept his agreement. Rick also agreed that, if he did
not keep his agreement, he would go to Gamblers
Anonymous.

Making the boundaries clear and measurable is part of
clarifying whether or not there is a difficulty. Making
agreements like Rick and Emily made can clarify the definition of a problem and what the next step will be for
clearing up the problem.

During this process of clarifying the boundaries of acceptable behavior, we help the couple avoid labeling each
other in a way that blames, invalidates, or closes down the
possibilities for change. We also help them avoid fighting
about the labels for the behavior.

A couple came in arguing about whether he was alcoholic or not. She, who had come from an "alcoholic"
family and was active in the Adult Children of Alco-
holics movement, claimed he was, and he just as adamantly claimed he wasn't. Bill was abashed to learn,
when he asked for a video description of what she
perceived as alcoholic, that the man did not drink at
all. She maintained that the behavior he showed was
indicative of being on a "dry drunk." He was
"grumpy" (spoke to her and the children in harsh
and loud voice tones), he isolated himself (he would
not talk to her for several days in a row), and he
would try to control her behavior (he would criticize
her for not cooking for the children when he was
working late). Once Bill got a description of these
behaviors, it was simply a matter of negotiating
changes in those behaviors. The husband never did
agree that he was alcoholic and the wife never

changed her opinion that he was. Still, they were able to make enough changes so that they stopped arguing about the matter.

We have stressed not blaming in this book, but that does not mean we let either partner off the hook for doing inappropriate behavior. We hold each person accountable for his or her actions. In the session, we resist invitations from either partner to blame or accept non-accountability.

We were working with a couple and found out that the husband had hit his wife. When we started to discuss the matter, the woman labeled the man a wife-beater. When she used the word, he responded by saying, "I slapped her. It was a reaction. It hurt me more than it hurt her." At this point, Bill interrupted and said, "Well, we could ask her opinion about that. But the main thing is that we all have to be satisfied that, whatever provocations happen, you will not hit her ever again." We then went on to discuss whether such safety was possible and what it would take to ensure no future violence.

The woman had labeled him in a way that closed down possibilities by saying, "He's a wife-beater." The man had invalidated his wife's experience by mind-reading and minimizing ("It hurt me more than it hurt her."). He had also talked about his violence in a non-accountable way ("I slapped her. It was a reaction."), implying that his wife's behavior had somehow *made* him get violent. The way we responded was intended to walk the fine line between blame, invalidation, and accountability. Blame is attributing bad intentions or bad traits to someone. Non-accountability is claiming that one is not responsible for one's behavior. Accountability is ensuring that each partner is held responsible as a personal agent for his or her actions.

Personal Power

When there have been actions that have disrupted the relationship, the question becomes what will steer the couple away from the dissolution of the relationship. Often the couple will have locked horns so that the big picture is obscured by the battle over inappropriate behaviors. We suggest to our clients, when confronting their partners about destructive behavior, that they point out how important the other person is to them, how much they love them, and how much they want to have their relationship endure the test of time. It is so powerful to say to someone, "I love you and I really need your help to stay in this relationship. That help is to not have gambling cause us such financial difficulties that my anxiety becomes too high to endure staying in this relationship." We think of this as using your personal power.

Lucy and Charles were close to breaking up over Charles's nightly stops at the bar with the guys after work. Lucy had already made it clear what she wanted: no driving after drinking. She came to us for help about what to do next with Charles. The relationship had become so strained that the word "love" had not been mentioned in a long time. We coached Lucy to write a letter emphasizing her caring for Charles her deep sadness at what seemed to be her losing him to alcohol, and her fear that he might not be alive much longer.

By coincidence Charles did have a car accident the week that she gave him the letter. Although no one was seriously hurt, the dose of reality along with Lucy's loving plea changed Charles's pattern. He stopped drinking and came in for therapy.

Consequences, Not Punishment

Even after the boundaries are clarified, sometimes the person continues to violate them. At that point we find ourselves coaching the distressed partner to give consequences for violations.

There is an important distinction between consequences and punishments. Punishment is delivered in anger and is an attempt to reform the person to whom it is directed. Since we don't orient our interventions toward fixing, reforming, or changing people's core or personality traits, we avoid punishment. We coach our clients to sit down calmly and tell the other person what the consequences will be and remind the out-of-line person that the goals are a loving relationship that has some safety and the preservation of the relationship.

Ellie and Butch had only been married one year. It was a second marriage for Ellie and a third for Butch. Ellie had met him right after he had come out of his second inpatient chemical dependency treatment program and he was maintaining his sobriety. Butch was an unemployed musician and Ellie had been a frugal factory worker who had maintained a house by herself for several years.

Butch's behavior became more and more out of line. He gave excuses for why he could not work and began smoking pot on a daily basis. Ellie began escalating consequences with our coaching. First, she refused to give him money, hoping that this would increase his motivation to at least get a job. When he began to write bad checks to get pot, she felt this was taking the meaning of the term "joint account" too far and closed the account.

Butch began taking her household possessions to the local pawnbroker in order to get money for drugs and began to combine pot with alcohol. At this point we encouraged her to separate from him.

Each of these escalating consequences was accompanied by very clear requests. These requests were about living drug-free, applying for jobs, and doing household tasks. Ellie had been very discouraged when she came home from work to find dog droppings on the floor that Butch refused to clean up even though these were his dogs and he was home all day. We were so careful about making sure that Butch knew what was expected that we had Ellie put her requests in writing.

Butch became more verbally abusive and eventually physically abusive. Ellie was still reluctant to divorce. Butch then got a job playing music in the South. Ellie felt some relief while Butch was gone and things looked more hopeful. At this point, Ellie learned that Butch was having an affair. She finally gave up and divorced him.

Consequences, as the above story demonstrates, will not always work to change the behavior of the person to whom they are applied. They do help establish clearly that the person who is doing the destructive or dangerous behavior is accountable. They also help move the partner out of a passive/victim position. After the divorce, we asked Ellie if she thought we should have pushed her to divorce sooner. She said she was glad she had tried so hard. It made her feel that she had done all she could for him and that she had nothing to feel guilty about as far as the divorce went. Ellie thanked us for sticking with her through all the ups and downs. Two years later she married a really fine man who was very loving to her.

Another couple we worked with had more success with this approach.

Frank and Tammy had been married for 12 years. Frank was physically abusive throughout the relationship and Tammy was ready to leave, in spite of the two children and the financial hardship she knew she would endure. They had separated twice and once had gotten to the day before divorce court, but Frank had always talked Tammy back into the relationship. In the session Tammy, with Frank there, promised us that if Frank ever touched her again in anger, the consequence would be that she would go through with the divorce without ever discussing it again with him. Frank was finally convinced of Tammy's intention to follow through if he ever got violent again and we heard from them a year later that he had not been abusive to her since that time.

Consequences are necessary when one partner continues to go beyond the line of what is considered acceptable. The top of our hierarchy of consequences is severing the relationship. We are very committed to saving relationships and have recommended divorce less than a dozen times. Since we have been doing therapy for over 15 years, it should be clear that we usually think there is hope. We are both firmly against violence and its continuing occurrence in a relationship has usually been our reason for recommending divorce. We strongly suggest that clients do not threaten divorce, but when the end of the rope is at hand, then it is fair play to be sure the other person understands where his or her behaviors are likely to lead.

Escalating Interventions for
Destructive/Harmful Behavior
in Relationships

1. Clarify the complaint and requests.

2. Change the patterns around the problem.

3. Clarify the limits of behavior and accountability.

4. Get the person who is requesting the change
to use personal power when requesting that the partner stay within limits.

5. Help the couple or the partner set and apply
consequences.

6. Get the boundary violator to make amends and
to reaffirm his/her commitment to staying within the
limits.

Making Amends

When the partner who has violated the boundaries in the
past is willing, we help him take some actions that can
mend the broken limits. The first is to acknowledge his
actions in the matter without making excuses. This is the
accountability piece. He does not have to accept blame,
just responsibility. The second repairing move is for the
violator to offer to make amends in some way or to restore
trust. The person might offer to go to a group for abusive
men or have the partner open all his mail for the next few

years to ensure that the person with whom he had the affair is not contacting him. One man offered to let his wife call him or drop in on him at any time when he was at work or any social event to reassure her that he was no longer lying to her about where he was (as he did when he had an affair). One woman wrote her partner an apology for having hit her and promised never to get physically violent again in the relationship. Sometimes such promises are merely empty words. For both of these women, the partner who wrote the letter and the one who received it, this was a meaningful apology and commitment. In other cases, it is important for the violator to establish the credibility of that renewed commitment over time with actions that stay within the boundaries.

Coaching People Who Have
Violated Boundaries
to Make Amends

1.   Get the person who violated the boundaries to acknowledge what he or she has done and not make excuses.

2.   Get the violator to offer to make amends or do something to restore trust. Let the person whose boundaries have been violated decide whether he or she even wants amends, and if so, what kind.

3.   Get the violator to recommit to the boundaries that have been agreed upon and show that commitment in action over time.

Individual Versus
Joint Sessions

We prefer to have the couple in a joint session while we are clarifying the limits and setting the consequences, but it is not essential. We believe that if one person changes his or her stance, that can shift what happens in the relationship. This even applies to destructive and harmful behavior. We often have only one person in our office—the one who is in danger or whose trust is constantly being betrayed or who does not like the partner's drinking or drug use. We take care not to imply that the person in our office has the problem or is part of the problem (as some systemic therapists believe). Our stance is that either person has the possibility of making a difference in a two-person relationship.

In general, then, when we encounter a very challenging couple, we start with the simple clarification of requests and limits, move up the hierarchy to using personal power and eventually to consequences, with the ultimate consequence being divorce. Only a small percentage of the couples we work with are so far over the edge. However, most therapists who work with couples will sooner or later need these tools.

9

CIRCLE THE WAGONS AND BEWARE THE TRIANGLE
Kids, Family, and Divorce

In this chapter, we take up some topics that are brought up in couples work, but not as commonly as the issues mentioned so far. These issues include setting boundaries with children and in-laws, and meeting the challenges of living in a stepfamily. We also take up the topic of divorce. While we work hard to avoid and prevent divorces, they inevitably occur in some cases. We offer some guidelines to make divorce and its aftereffects more manageable and less destructive.

We take care not to impose our stories and values on the couples we work with. Nevertheless, we have noticed some general strategies that can help couples avoid or clear up typical issues involving kids, extended families, and divorce. There are two general themes that run through this chapter. The first is avoiding the triangle, and the second is distinguishing between the marital rela-

tionship and the parental relationship or other family relationships.

Beware the Triangle

A triangle in this context means three people. When we
say "beware the triangle," we mean avoid as much as
possible delivering a message to someone through a third
party. If you've ever played the party game called Gossip,
you have gotten a glimpse into the problem of the triangle.
In this game, someone whispers a message into the ear of
the person next to her. That person in turn whispers the
same message into the ear of the next person. When the
message gets to the last person, he or she repeats it out
loud. Inevitably, the message has gotten distorted in the
repetition. So the first problem with the triangle is that
messages often get distorted or changed when they take a
roundabout route.

The second difficulty with the triangle is that the person
in the middle usually feels divided loyalties. When one
parent sends the child to the other parent's new home to
spy and report back on the ex-spouse's new date, the child
is going to feel some conflict about this.

So we try to get people to communicate and interact
directly with one another and avoid the triangle.

Keep the Marital
Relationship Separate
from the Family/
Parental Relationship

Time and time again we have seen couples in which, once
the children came along, problems started in the marriage.
One of the ways to avoid such problems is to draw clear

boundaries around the marital relationship. This can be accomplished by having the couple spend time together without the children, having the couple put locks on the bedroom door, encouraging the parents to take trips away from home and the children, arranging for the couple to jointly agree on the rules for the children, etc. Usually, then, what we help couples do is to draw the wagons of their marital relationship into a circle and guard that relationship from intrusion from outside forces (children, family of origin members, work, household duties, etc.). Keeping this boundary clear can even help after the dissolution of the marriage. During divorces, it is important to keep in mind that the parental relationship will continue while the marital one will not.

Parenting and Partnering

We know a therapist who teaches classes on how to have your marriage survive parenthood. That idea that marriages are strained by children fits with our experience as therapists and as parents. Couples often neglect their relationships by focusing upon children rather than taking the time to balance the demands of parenthood with those of marriage. When both parents work outside the home, the guilt of having had the child in day-care or intense fatigue make going out as a couple much less likely.

The most extreme lack of marital boundaries we ever encountered was a couple who had an only child, a 10-year-old daughter. (Speaking from our personal and professional experience, it is easier for an only child to get overly involved in the parents' marriage.) If the parents tried to go out for an evening without the daughter, she would lie down in the driveway to prevent their departure. This little girl asked a question that would surely win an award for the most enmeshed question of the year: When she discovered that it was almost her parents' wedding anniversary, she asked, "Where are we going for our anniversary?"

With this couple we focused on tasks to help them clarify and separate the parental relationship from their marital relationship, including spending some special couple time outside the house together each week. We helped them find activities that the daughter wanted to do (things like going skating with friends and taking dance lessons) and arrange for those activities to happen on nights when they went out on dates. This had the effects of getting the child involved with peers, normalizing her social life, and easing the parents back into time without her.

Although we have experienced similar problems with couples having more than one child, another single-child family had similar difficulties.

Kay and Jack had divorced and were considering giving the marriage a second try. They had one child, Tracy, 11 years old, whom the mother had confided in through the divorce process. Jack had had an affair and this had precipitated the divorce. Kay had discussed the affair at length with Tracy. Naturally she had not painted a pretty picture. Jack complained that Tracy was present for every conversation that Kay and Jack had and that the girl was expressing strong negative opinions about her mother's dating her father again. All of us agreed that if there were to be even an opportunity to begin working on the marriage, there would have to be an elimination of Tracy's involvement in the marriage. This was accomplished in two ways. We coached Kay to tell Tracy that her opinions about what her dad and mom did about the marriage were not to be discussed. Kay was to say that she already understood Tracy's opinion and that she would keep it in mind, but that Kay did not intend to continue discussing the topic. Jack asked, and Kay agreed, that if he called on the phone Kay was to take the call in a room where Tracy was not present so that they could have a private conversation. These were just the beginning steps but a prerequisite to successful therapy.

The second way that we see parenting as a marital issue is that parents often disagree about what is expected of the children and how to discipline them.

Mary and Mark had a large family, seven children, all still at home. There were two areas of conflict that needed to be resolved: how to get agreement on the rules for the kids and how to include Mark as a parent. The children and their mother were usually in one camp and the father, who had a quick temper, was in another. This division was inconsistent with Mary's fundamentalist religious philosophy, which stressed honoring the husband, and that made changing a little easier.

Both parents felt the children were verging on being out of control. We asked when they had felt more successful with the children as a group and found that written rules had worked better. Therefore, we negotiated an assignment with the parents: They were to schedule a time outside of the home without the children present (such as in a restaurant or a park). They were to sit together and prepare a set of rules for the children with consequences if these rules were not followed. This had the dual effect of getting them on the same team and giving them time alone, away from the children.

Often spouses will resolve their marital conflict and then want to come for one extra session to talk about parenting issues.

Sometimes parents ask for guidelines about rules. For us this is pretty simple: Have as few rules as possible, make most of the rules about consideration of others' space and property, and make the most severe consequences for anything that is life-threatening, such as playing with matches, or later, driving drunk.

Nearly all of the principles that we apply to couples work can be applied to parenting issues. One example of the concept of asking for a change of actions instead of a change in experience occurred when Bill was working with a family in which the parents were dissatisfied with the behavior of their teenage son.

The parents felt upset at the deplorable condition of their son's room. The parents had gone round and round with their son on this issue, to no avail. Bill discovered that none of them had a clear picture of what a clean room looked like and precisely when it was supposed to be clean. Bill led them to more and more detailed video descriptions of what they wanted, arriving at an agreement that the son would remove all of the dirty clothes from his room, hang up or put away all of the clean clothes, and change the sheets, vacuum, and dust once a week. It was agreed that he was to do these tasks on Friday by 4:30 p.m. and that he could not leave for the evening until these tasks were done. As the family started to leave, the mother said, "Yes, but I want him to *want* to clean his room.'' Bill assured her that as a man nearing 30 (this was some years ago), he still did not want to clean his room. ''Let's just get him to clean his room. Perhaps by the time *he's* 30, he'll *want* to clean it.''

Pat's doctoral dissertation was on marital satisfaction. From reviewing the literature it is abundantly clear that having children, particularly school-age children, is negatively correlated with reports of marital happiness. The challenge of preserving the marriage while parenting can be magnified when the children are not biologically both parents' children.

Stepparenting and Blended Families

When Bill faced the prospect of becoming a stepfather, he already knew three ways of being a stepparent that did not work. The first was to come into the family and let everyone know that he thought Pat and her first husband had screwed these kids up and he was now here to set things right. The second unworkable model was to try to be an instant buddy with the children. ''We're all just one big happy family now. We *love* each other.'' The children often feel forced, in order to appease their biological parent, to go along with this charade, but under the surface they don't feel instant love. The third unworkable model was to talk to the biological parent about what you like and don't like about the kids. This is the triangle approach. We have already discussed the unworkable aspects of this strategy.

Since Bill knew what didn't work, he searched for some model that could work. The model that he selected for his role as stepfather was roommate. What he asked of the kids and what he tried to give to them was ''good roommate behavior." Good roommates do not mess with each other's property without permission, they keep common areas clean, they are considerate about sharing common property, such as the telephone and they don't make loud invasive noises while the roommate is trying to do something of a quiet nature. When we are working with stepfamilies—or any families with older children—we often tell them how that approach worked satisfactorily for us.

There was a second piece that was also important for us, and we share this with stepfamilies as well. This is the issue of avoiding the triangle. As we mentioned at the beginning of this chapter, passing messages is called triangulation. In our own family we had a chance to deal with the triangle with our oldest son, Nick. Nick is now in his twenties and has turned out wonderfully, but for a while he was justifiably a winner on the debate team! We are all musical and there was sometimes competition to see who got to use the great musical equipment. Bill would be upset if Nick, as a teenager, would leave the equipment on. We quickly learned that Pat would feel crushed under the burden of being the conduit (corner of the triangle) for messages between the two of them. Nick and Bill began to communicate directly and Pat could stay out of it. That helped everyone.

The issue of boundaries can be a problem in any family but becomes magnified by a stepfamily environment.

Craig and Sandy had been married for two years when Craig's daughter in her early twenties, Cherise, boomeranged back into the home. (The present generation of young adults has been called the "baby boomerangers" because they keep coming back to their parents' homes.) The difficulties were probably made worse by Sandy's not having had children, so her tolerance was lower than it might have been.

Craig had felt very guilty about the children, mostly for picking such a weird woman to mate with in the first place. He had had custody of the two girls for most of their childhoods.

Now Sandy was at her wits' end. She was a tidy person who was upset by the chaos that had resulted from Cherise's return, which had no end in sight. We helped them avoid arguing about who was right or wrong and negotiated agreements with Craig about how long Cherise would be there, what they were financially responsible for, and what Craig agreed to ask of Cherise in exchange for free room and board.

Craig asked Cherise to cook one meal a week, take out the garbage once a week, and launder all the used towels once a week in exchange for free room and board. These arrangements appeased Sandy. Cherise moved out in two months, which was a relief to all parties.

Boundary issues have to do with who lives where, when, who is allowed to give input on what issues, who is present in certain locations (such as the parents' bedroom), and how time is spent.

Alan and Nancy were each in their third marriage. Nancy's grown son moved in just a month before things escalated to such a degree that they came for therapy. Nancy said that Alan communicated his distaste about having the children around by acting "grumpy." We got a video description of what "grumpy" looked like, which was primarily voice tone, and a request about what Nancy would like to see happen instead. Nancy requested that Alan use more courteous words such as "please" and "thank you" and a different voice tone.

One of the stories we told them was about the early
stages in our stepfamily. Pat thought Bill was being a
bit critical of Zack, her youngest son. Bill was not
sure he agreed that he was being critical, but asked
Pat what she would like him to do. Pat asked Bill to
give Zack at least one compliment a day. Bill agreed
and said that would be easy because Zack was such a
good kid. Hearing Pat's story, Nancy got the message
that labeling Alan and preaching at him was not going
to solve the difficulty and began focusing on requests.

We sometimes joke with couples that if we are a
blended family then we need to be put through the
blender a little longer because we are still a little lumpy.
Actually, things have become pretty smooth for us with
the passage of time, but there was enough conflict to give
us a lot of empathy for the difficulties couples can experience while creating stepfamilies.

Problems With Families
of Origin

We have found that the principles mentioned about children apply equally well to dealing with each partner's family of origin: Set appropriate boundaries, communicate
about facts not stories, ask for what you want, avoid trian-
gulations, and change the patterns.

Rayne and Luke were in frequent contact with Luke's
family because they were participating in a family
farm. Luke's mother offered Rayne advice about how
to decorate the house that had been the mother-in-
law's, how to raise children, and how to run the
household. Rayne's pattern was to keep her upset
feelings to herself around her mother-in-law but to

berate Luke for his mother's behavior. We did three main things: We supported Rayne in changing her pattern by discussing what she was upset about directly with her mother-in-law, handling this in a tactful way by first acknowledging the woman's good intentions. We got the couple to agree to set some time boundaries, because the mother-in-law would drop over at any time. (The couple agreed to ask the mother-in-law to not drop over after 7:30 p.m., as that was their family time.) We coached Rayne to make her requests in videotalk, so that she could be certain whether or not she was getting the results she wanted with her mother-in-law.

Avoiding a Bloody Divorce

Unabashed Marriage Savers

We make no apologies for being unabashed marriage savers (Weiner-Davis, 1987). Our stance is that people come into our office trying to figure out how to make their marriages work and to stay together. We operate on this assumption until we learn otherwise or until it is obvious to us and the couple that there is no hope of staying together. Nevertheless, we do take precautions to assure everyone's safety. Even in cases in which there has been physical violence, we believe that the couple can often stay together. While we do not feel that divorce has to be bad, hurtful, and unnecessary, most people (and their kids) do hurt miserably going through it.

Many times therapists give up too quickly on couples or say things that seed the idea of divorce in the spouses' minds. We mentioned earlier the couple who came to us after seeing a therapist who had said, after only one family

session and a session with their son, "I don't want to drop
a bomb, but I think that maybe you two just don't want to
be married." It took us three sessions to repair the damage
from that statement. Having supervised other therapists
for many years, we have found that some, particularly
those who have not experienced the misery of divorce,
are blasé about making statements that encourage people
to give up. Are you inviting the spouses to hang in there
or are you planting ideas that give permission to give up?
Sometimes recording your own sessions and listening to
them can help you notice what you are saying and avoid
being an inadvertent marriage discourager.

We understand, however, from both personal and professional experience, the enough-is-enough point that can
be reached. We each had relatively amiable divorces, using
only one attorney in both cases. Others have not had such
an easy time with their divorces. When the divorce threat-
ens to get bitter, we have several suggestions.

The first and foremost suggestion is to help couples stay
out of the past and focus instead on the present and the
future. They are probably never going to resolve the old
marital issues and trying to do so typically leads to further
conflicts. We have seen people try to get an understanding
of themselves by asking their ex-spouse's viewpoint. That
is not a good place to search for accurate input. Instead
we help clients make requests for future behavior they
would like from the ex-spouse. We recommend limiting
these requests to areas that are still relevant after the dissolution of the marital relationship, such as joint financial
matters, the health, welfare, and education of the children, and legal matters. All other topics should be taboo.

Shirley and Ken had been divorced for over a year
but the skirmishes continued and were beginning to
take a toll on their two children, who were repeat-

edly dragged into the conflict. We proposed to Shirley, who was the only one willing to come in for therapy, that she make a point of not having discussions with the children about the conflicts with their dad. We also helped her coach the children to say to their dad, when some issue that had to do with her was brought up, "Why don't you talk to mom about that?"

Under the guise of discussing the children, Ken would go back to old marital issues. He would analyze the children's current problems in terms of Shirley's family and character. We coached Shirley not to take the bait. We suggested she just say that, unless he had some request about actions he wanted her to take, she was not willing to discuss his theories about their children's behavior. As a reminder she put a note on the phone saying, "Health, Education, Visitation of the Children." This helped her avoid getting into those unproductive conversations.

Next, the healing ceremonies we suggested in Chapter 6 can be useful in helping the parties involved leave the past relationship or issues behind and move on. Sometimes problems arise because someone is unfinished with the marriage or some marital issues. Rituals can help bring those issues to a close.

As therapists we often feel a sense of loss and failure when a couple divorces, except in the case of extremely inappropriate behavior on the part of one spouse. One of the comforts that we offer is that there would not have been any way that either of us could have been as happy as we are now without having gone through that process. Only time will tell for certain whether or not the couples who got a divorce found a happier life and considered the divorce a success.

10

WHY SHOULD YOUR VAGINA BE DIFFERENT FROM YOUR EAR?

Intimacy and Sex

Since intimacy and sex are such crucial issues for many of the couples we see, we have decided to devote a chapter just to these special areas.

Creating Intimacy

"Intimacy" is one of those packaged words we mentioned earlier. It means different things to different people. When intimacy is mentioned as a primary complaint, we ask each partner for a video description of intimacy. For some, it is talking, for others, touching is crucial. Someone once said that for a woman to want sex, she has to feel intimacy; for a man to feel intimate, he has to have sex. That's a bit too generalized for us (and doesn't explain why some same-sex couples experience similar disparities), but perhaps it points to one of the sources of the intimacy difficulties that couples experience. People often have different requirements for intimacy and don't realize that their partners may not share their views.

We ask questions that elicit a video description and at the same time create a positive expectation for beginning to achieve intimacy. "What will you be doing when you are feeling close to each other again?"

> Elizabeth and Roger had been married for 12 years. They had careers that were consuming and two children (5 and 7 years old). They both complained that they didn't feel close and, even though they weren't approaching divorce, they knew things were deteriorating between them. It was difficult for them to recall what had been happening in their relationship when they had been close. When they did identify lying in bed and making love until mid-morning, they felt more discouraged because they could not imagine doing that with the kids in the house. However, in response to our query about what they *would* be doing when they felt closer to each other, they gave us enough specifics to help them devise ways to achieve that closeness. We devised two plans: One was to set things up so that the kids would leave them alone for at least a little while on Saturday. This involved leaving a small manageable pitcher of milk, two bowls and spoons where the children could reach them, renting a videotape that could only be watched on Saturday morning, and then discussing the plan with the children. The second plan was to go for an overnight, weekend package at a local hotel, arranging for the sitter to stay with the children. Both of these arrangements worked well for creating a context for intimacy.

The Martian's Guide to Intimacy

While each partner and couple has idiosyncratic ideas about what constitutes intimacy, we have found some general elements of intimacy that hold true for most people in this culture. We often use these general principles to help clients articulate their own unique definition of intimacy. We call this "The Martian's Guide to Intimacy," as it seeks to answer the question: What would a Martian who came to Earth to study Earthlings doing intimacy find?

First, our Martian anthropologist would notice that people who are intimate spend time together. You may remember that, when you started a job, you thought there was no one there to whom you could become close. After working with those people daily for months, however, you may have become close to one or more of them. (That is one of the ways affairs get started. The luxury of time to talk and interact is often more available at work than at home.)

Second, the Martian would notice that people who are intimate talk about certain types of things—vulnerable feelings, hopes, and dreams. We've noticed that men typically do not share their vulnerable feelings (such as fear, hurt, or embarrassment), but instead specialize in showing only one emotion: anger. Encouraging people, particularly men, to talk about what scares them and what hurts them often helps couples move to more intimate connections. Talking about hopes and dreams for the future or even hopes and dreams from the past can also show this vulnerability. If you shared with someone that you had always wanted to be a missionary and that person snorted, "You! Are you kidding?" it would be a good hint that this person was not a good candidate for intimacy. In an intimate relationship, when vulnerable feelings, hopes, and dreams are shared, there is a sense that they will be cherished, not ridiculed.

The third observation that our Martian could make is that in intimate relationships there is a fair amount of affectionate touching. People who feel close typically touch each other. If it is a sexual relationship then there is sexual touching as well.

To help couples achieve intimacy, we emphasize two overall tasks: Remove the barriers to intimacy (like blame, invalidation, and unhelpful/destructive patterns) and help the couple do the actions that can create intimacy.

When Carole and Dennis came in for a session, one could almost hear a wind whistling in the wasteland of their relationship. They didn't fight much; they didn't seem to have enough emotional contact to fight. They defined their problem as not feeling close. We first arranged for them to have time together, then we focused on intimacy-creating behaviors.

Since it had been six months since they had had sex, we started by asking them to give each other foot and hand massages, to get their touching going again. This was particularly helpful to Dennis, because he reported that he had felt closest in the past when he had had physical contact with Carole. She remembered they had had more eye contact when they had felt closer earlier in the relationship, so we had them face one another for 15 minutes a day and talk.

After these initial tasks had helped them start feeling a bit closer to one another, we had them interview each other as though they were going to write biographies about each other. We have noticed that when people first get close, one of the ways they do it is to find out about each other's past, their childhoods, their first loves, etc. This exercise also helped them move in the direction of closeness.

In this case, we used our Martian's guide concepts, as well as one of the couple's idiosyncratic elements of intimacy. Eye contact, which Carole taught us was an important action component of closeness for her, helped this couple find a unique way of creating intimacy.

Martian's Guide to Intimacy

• Affiliation. Spending time together without others around.

• Talking with one's partner about vulnerable feelings, memories, hopes and dreams.

• Affectionate touching.

Trouble in the area of intimacy is often a part of the sexual difficulties people experience. Consequently helping people feel more intimate often resolves sexual difficulties. Many couples tell us that when they are getting along better in general, they have a better sexual relationship. At times, however, sexual issues need to be addressed separately.

Sexual Issues

Sexual Complaints, Requests, and Praise

Everything we have said about good communication applies to creating a good sexual relationship: Get people to tell each other when the partner is doing something they do not like (sexual complaints); get them to ask for what they want sexually (sexual requests); and get them to let the partner know when they are doing something sexual they like (sexual praise). Of course, we get them to do this in a way that does not blame, invalidate, or close down the possibilities for change.

One barrier to accomplishing clear communication about sex arises because we make sex such a weird thing in our culture. Part of the problem is a vocabulary difficulty. When discussing sexual matters, we use either street language or language that sounds like a med school course ("place your digit upon my labia"). It is difficult for many couples to talk about "down there."

THE PLEASURE TEACHING SESSION

Since many couples we see have not ever communicated clearly about what they want (and don't want) sexually, we recommend an in vivo training session—a pleasure teaching session (Newhorn, 1973). The couple is to set aside at least a half-hour. One person then does a variety of touching and sexual stimulation to the other person. The person receiving the stimulation is to give feedback, such as "harder, softer, move your tongue (fingers, etc.) slower (faster, etc.)." We joke with people that if they are too inhibited to say what they want out loud, perhaps they can use our special signal system. We call this the Hudson-O'Hanlon Squeeze Technique (as opposed to the Masters and Johnson Squeeze Technique). The pleasure receiver is to squeeze the pleasure giver's right arm to signal "I like that. Do more of that," and to squeeze the pleasure giver's left arm to indicate that he or she wants less of that kind of stimulation.

Pat tells couples working on these issues, "Either the two of you start communicating about this at home, or you are going to have to talk about your sexual preferences during a session with me." Most people are inhibited enough that giving them that warning increases their motivation to begin communicating with each other about what they want and don't want.

Bill and his first couple of sexual partners, all shy people, never talked about sex during or after the act. Consequently, he never knew if he was doing anything right or wrong, or even if those partners had orgasms. He assumed that they must have liked the sex a little because they did seem to want to have sex again. Then he began a relationship with a woman who, the first time they had sex, said things like "Put your hand here," and "Does that feel good? Should I do more of that?" Bill was in a state of shock. He thought to himself, "You mean people can talk during this?" Pat is grateful to this woman because her talking ended up ultimately contributing to Pat's sexual relationship with Bill.

MIX 'N' MATCH SEXUAL MENU

Another strategy we use with couples is to get them to be more creative about sex. This involves creating a mix 'n' match menu of sexual behavior. Specifically, we draw two columns, one of the doers and one of the doees of sexual behavior. The doers are any parts of the body that have muscles that can initiate stimulation. The doees are the parts of the body that can receive stimulation. We then suggest that the couple match items from column A with items from column B. It is a Chinese restaurant menu way for couples to begin to communicate about their likes and dislikes and to become more creative about their sex life.

Dysfunctions

Vaginismus (an involuntary tightening of the vaginal muscles that makes penetration painful or impossible), erectile difficulties, non-orgasmic problems, or phobias are com-

Doers	Doees	
Fingers	Mouth	
Tongue	Clitoris	
Mouth	Penis	
Penis	Vagina	One couple's
Vagina	Breast	menu selections
Hand	Nipples	
	Anus	
	Skin	

Doers	Doees	
Fingers	Mouth	
Tongue	Clitoris	
Mouth	Penis	
Penis	Vagina	Another couple's
Vagina	Breast	menu selections
Hand	Nipples	
	Anus	
	Skin	

mon sexual dysfunctions. We tend to combine individual and couples work with these issues. Hypnosis is one of our personal favorite treatment methods. We won't detail this work here, as it is more individually-based and has been covered elsewhere (O'Hanlon & Martin, 1992).

When couples complain of sexual dysfunctions, we have some general strategies. The first is very traditional sex therapy: progressive nondemand touching to help the partners get back to their natural feelings of sexual excitement. Assignments would start with a pleasure teaching session that did not involve breasts and genitals and progress to full pleasure teaching sessions that involved breasts and genitals. The important principle here is to separate the pressure to perform (to have an orgasm or to have and maintain an erection) from the experience of being touched and aroused.

The techniques that we have used elsewhere can greatly contribute to this: video talk, changing patterns (perhaps not touching genitals or breasts outside the bedroom, which turns some women off), and negotiating agreements about sexual interaction.

Cheryl and Todd had been married for some years. Cheryl had progressively become non-orgasmic. She felt that the reason was that Todd would frequently grab her breasts or stick his hand down her pants in situations where she could not, or did not want to, respond. Todd agreed to make sure that any time he touched Cheryl outside the bedroom, he would not include breasts and genitals or even innuendo statements. After a couple of weeks of Todd's keeping his word about this, Cheryl was ready to move to the pleasure teaching session.

Sometimes part of changing a sexual relationship will involve healing from a past traumatic time in the relationship.

Sam and Betty had been married for 12 years. Sam was in the military and Betty was a homemaker. At the beginning of the relationship, before their children were born, they had sex four times a day. About the same time that they had their first child, Sam was on a remote tour of duty (gone) for most of a year. When he returned, Betty became drastically turned off by sex. That conflict eventually became the focus of their relationship. They had had previous counseling, during which there was some improvement, but now they were in conflict again. Betty came to see

Pat first, asking for hypnosis to see if there were any underlying causes to her disinterest, such as forgotten childhood sexual abuse.

In hypnosis it came to light that the barrier to Betty's being able to discover her own rhythm of sexual interest was two times she had felt used and depersonalized by Sam. Pat had Betty imagine these two times as though she were watching a movie. Betty could then imagine them being contained on that reel of movie film. When, while Betty was in trance, Pat suggested that these could be destroyed in a fire, Betty seemed hesitant. She said, "I think I want to drive over them first." Pat led her through images of first driving over the film and them taking the scraps and throwing them into the fire.

The following week Pat met with Sam and Betty. Pat suggested a ceremony that Betty and Sam might do together to help heal from this event. Sam was to write a letter asking Betty to forgive him and Betty was to write a letter about how much these events upset her. They were to carry these for a week and then have a ceremony burning or burying the letters together followed by a celebratory dinner. Pat also talked about pattern changes, particularly that Sam would use nonsexual touching outside the bedroom and conversation to create the likelihood that Betty would be interested in sex later.

Sometimes a dysfunction can be of such a prolonged nature that even hypnosis and pattern intervention techniques will not help.

Pat was seeing Doris and Harlan. They had been married for 35 years, and Harlan had in all this time been a premature ejaculator. He had never been able to

sustain an erection without ejaculating for longer that
two minutes. We did hypnosis and pleasure teaching
session assignments with them, but the problem re-
mained the same. We encouraged them to use alternative methods for Doris to receive pleasure. Harlan
continued to ejaculate quickly, but they were able to
create a more satisfying sexual relationship.

The Tyranny of the Big O and Intercourse

We were in a staff meeting when one of the other therapists mentioned working with a couple where the husband
had been on blood pressure medication for some time and
therefore had not been able to get an erection. The therapist said that the husband and the wife had stopped having
sex with each other. Bill spoke up and asked, ''Well don't
his fingers and tongue still work?'' Sex can be so much
more that penis-vaginal contact. This is important to teach
couples. We often encourage them to include masturbation, oral and manual stimulation in their sexual relationship, whether or not erectile difficulties are a factor.

We feel that masturbation can add to a relationship, not
take away from it, as long as one partner doesn't routinely
masturbate and become disinterested in sexual interaction
when the other partner wants sexual contact. The idea
that two people are always going to be in sync sexually is
a little ludicrous.

Another idea that creates unrealistic expectations is that
when couples have sex, both must have orgasms (The
Big O) every time. Of course, if one is not having orgasms
at all, this can be a concern, but occasionally one partner
may not have an orgasm and still enjoy the sexual experience. We try to unhook people from the demand to have
orgasms. At the same time, it is not unrealistic to be able
to have simultaneous orgasms (both partners climaxing

at the same time). With good communication, it is possible to synchronize orgasms at times. Again, the point is to remove the demand factor and communicate about what you like and don't like.

Normalizing

Our main goal is to normalize sex. When Pat was doing co-therapy with a couple for a sexual problem, her co-therapist said to the female client, "Why should your vagina be any different from your ear?" In truth the difference is that you will not get arrested for going out in public with your ear exposed. The point is that most people treat sexual areas of the body as if they were weird and not to be spoken about.

Bill used normalizing effectively with a man who initially sought help in reducing his high blood pressure. He also mentioned casually in the first few minutes that maybe the high blood pressure was causing the impotence he had recently been experiencing. After several sessions, his blood pressure was down and he was satisfied that it would remain so. Bill asked if there was anything else that he was concerned about. He then discussed his concern about his impotence, a topic he had felt too embarrassed to emphasize at first, but which was really a bigger concern than the high blood pressure. Bill talked with him about the possibility of doing hypnosis for this and/or participating in therapy with his wife.

In the course of this discussion, Bill mentioned that this was a common occurrence for men. In fact, Bill himself had been impotent at times and had found that, the more he worried about it, the worse it got. Finally, he knew enough to just relax and concentrate on enjoying himself sexually, rather than striving to get an erection. He had not had the problem for any length of time since then.

When the man came back for the next session, he said that hypnosis was unnecessary because he no longer had a problem with impotence. When asked what had made the difference, he said that hearing that Bill had had the same problem made him feel it wasn't really irreversible and that he wasn't as strange as he had thought he was. When Bill happened to meet the man and his wife several months later, she blushed and thanked Bill for the help he had given her husband, leaving Bill with the impression that things had continued in a positive direction.

Dealing With
Sexual Boredom

Couples commonly complain that they haven't been having sex frequently enough. It is so easy for long-term married couples to fall into a pattern of doing sex the same way at the same time. We often prescribe the mix 'n' match menu mentioned earlier changes in location (moving from the bedroom to other rooms in the house to have sex or having sex in places outside the house); changes in clothing (many couples take off their clothes, get in bed and have sex—this is different from their courting patterns of taking off each other's clothes as part of the sexual interaction or we might suggest that they wear different clothes, costumes, etc.); reading or sharing erotic fantasies with each other, etc.

We basically focus on getting video descriptions of the partners' repetitive patterns of sexual interaction and coach them to introduce variations where regularities have been. Again, we avoid letting the couple spin causal theories or give labels that close down the possibilities for change.

Sexual Identity Issues

A man once came to Bill in a very agitated state. When Bill asked what his trouble was, the man replied earnestly and desperately, "I'm a latent homosexual!" Bill, not appreciating this type of popular Freudian self-diagnosis, replied, just as earnestly, "You are a latent many things: a latent dog, a latent president of the United States. What makes you think you'll turn into a homosexual?" The man reported that, while he was having sex with his wife, he had lately been having fantasies of nude men. These fantasies had grown in intensity until they dominated his attention during sex with his wife. He feared he was on the road to becoming homosexual. Bill asked the man if he wanted to do homosexual things. He adamantly assured Bill that he was seeking help because he did not want to act on these fantasies, although deep down he feared he would. Bill said that if the man decided that he wanted to do homosexual things, Bill would help him come to terms with that, but he had heard nothing to indicate the man was homosexual.

The man was amazed. "What about these fantasies?" he asked. Bill explained that there is a difference between fantasy and action and between fantasy and identity. Perhaps these fantasies were a message from deep inside about his real desires, but perhaps they were just random fantasies. Bill said that he had a guess that they had happened infrequently at first and that the more the man had tried to get rid of them, the more intense and frequent they became. The man agreed that this fit the facts. Bill recommended an experiment. Every time he started to make love with his wife, and even at random times during the day when he had a moment, he should try to make the nude men fantasies happen. A week of diligently practicing this exercise convinced the man that, the more he encouraged the fantasies, the less they ran the show.

This story illustrates two of our basic stances: Experience is experience and does not determine identity; fantasies are fantasies and do not have to control action. While it has been empowering for some to "come out of the closet" (publicly declare their homosexuality), for others making a firm decision about sexual identity is a confusing, disempowering process. Labeling oneself sometimes closes down options. Research and many years of practice indicate that many "heterosexuals" have had homosexual activities in their lives and many "homosexuals" have had heterosexual experiences in their lives. Doing is doing and being is being. Neither one has to determine the other. In each case, we try to help our clients sort out whether making a decision (or public declaration) about being homosexual would serve them well or not.

This is not to diminish the sometimes difficult struggle that people who choose (or find themselves in) a homosexual life go through. There are many prejudices and awkward social situations to be dealt with. For therapists there are many special issues with homosexual couples that can only be learned from experience with them as clients (Carl, 1990). Nevertheless, without seeming too overconfident, we think that our model is generic enough so that it can be used without much trouble with same-sex as well as heterosexual couples.

A young man who was struggling to break free from his family of origin came in after talking seriously about committing suicide It took a few sessions for the man to bring up his concerns, but he finally cautiously floated the idea that he had always been attracted to men. When we explored this issue, he finally decided that he was gay. His suicidal thoughts and feelings left as soon as he came to this decision. He was able to tell some members of his family of origin and decided that there were others who would not accept the news and that it was none of their business.

Another case showed some of the special concerns of same-sex couples.

Andy was in a long-term lesbian relationship. She came for help in changing some patterns that she and her partner, Ruth, had fallen into. They would constantly fight about money. Ruth, who did not come to the session, had a great deal of money from a business she had sold some years earlier. When the two would discuss plans for their house or some other major joint projects, Andy would get upset, knowing that she could not pull her weight financially and provide half the money for the project. Ruth felt this rule was silly because she did not mind giving more than 50% to their joint expenses and projects. Ruth was frustrated because she wanted to do more household improvements, but would have to wait for several years for Andy to save up the money to pay her half. Bill asked Andy what she was so concerned about, since Ruth clearly indicated that she did not mind paying more than 50%. Because they had no legal sanction for the relationship (i.e., a marriage license), Andy felt as if Ruth would feel ripped off if they ever separated (as there would be no court proceedings to help them determine a fair settlement). Andy was afraid Ruth would blame her later. During the session, we worked out a plan in which every time Ruth put up more than half the money for a project, she would sign an agreement not to blame Andy ever in the future, as she was giving this money of her own free will. Andy was amused by this plan, Ruth agreed to it, and soon the two were able to make money plans without the old conflicts.

Model Openness in Communicating About Sex

Once Bill was in Ireland teaching about this approach to sexuality. In the audience were several nuns, one of whom was a spry 70-year-old. When he got to the part about getting couples to discuss their sexual preferences openly and frankly, many of the participants in the room became noticeably uncomfortable. How could Bill talk so openly about sexuality in front of the nuns? Since the nuns were sitting in the back of the room, Bill could see what the other participants could not: The nuns were nodding and smiling during the discussion. At the end of the class, the 70-year-old nun spoke up and said, "That's just the same way I talk to couples about sex. We must help them speak openly about these matters. We have no official divorce here in Ireland, but a lot of separation and many miserable marriages. If we are to help these couples stay together and be happy, we have to help them communicate about sex."

We want to encourage you to be as open with your clients as this nun was. Model for them that talking about sex is okay and that asking for what you want is a prerequisite to a great sexual relationship. Often couples tell us that they have frankly talked about their sexual preferences and dislikes for the first time in our office or between sessions. Our basic value is that anything couples want to do with each other that they can agree upon and that will not result in bodily harm is fine.

We also apply the methods of our general model to the couple's sexual relationship. Make requests and complaints that are specific. Give specific comments on what works for you. Avoid labels that close down possibilities, blame, or invalidate.

11

RELATIONSHIP GLUE
Eliciting Love and Commitment

Sometimes partners seem so bitter towards each other that it is hard to believe that they were ever in love. They may arrive in the therapist's office doubting whether they love each other. Therefore, we usually avoid asking questions about love and commitment at the outset of marital therapy. We are well aware that stories can and do change during therapy. One of the stories that changes dramatically depending on whether things are going well in the relationship or not is the *love* part of the love story.

Before we focus on love, we usually do all the things we have discussed in earlier sections of this book. That includes clearing up difficulties, miscommunications, destructive interactions, and unfinished business. When one or both partners express their doubts about being in love, we usually give them an analogy: "When you first fell in love, it was as if there was a golden light that shone on both of you—the golden light of love. As time went on, misunderstandings, hurts, and conflicts threw manure on the light, until it was so obscured that you weren't sure there was any light left. Our task in therapy, then, is to wash away the manure and find out whether the golden light is still there. It may not be, but often we find that it is there, just covered over by conflicts and hurt. So let's not make any decisions about love until we clear away the problems.''

Maps of Loveland, or What Does Love Look Like?

When we first got together, we discovered that each of us had different ideas about what constitutes a "good gift." Pat wanted something that was a surprise, even if it did not fit or wasn't exactly what she would have picked out for herself. The element of surprise was the key to her satisfaction. Bill, however, wanted something that he had previously indicated he wanted. At first, Pat would buy Bill surprises and then watch with disappointment as he tried to look appreciative. Bill would get Pat something she had said she wanted and then learn that she was disappointed because it was not a surprise.

The same is true in dealing with love. One of the challenges of love is to recognize that your partner may have a different map of love than you have. The first task is to get a videotalk equivalent for what constitutes love for each partner. What does love look like and sound like for that person?

Once a map of each person's "loveland" is obtained, the second task is to get each to acknowledge that the other's map is valid. The reader may recall an earlier case in which the husband thought love involved picnics and the wife thought it involved cleaning whiskers from the sink. The first challenge with this couple was to get each to realize that his or her picture was not the "right" picture of love, only one of the many possible.

The third task is to get each partner to do more of what looks like love to the partner.

A couple on the verge of a divorce came to see Bill. The man had been a drinker and had recently stopped drinking. His wife had expected that many of their problems would clear up when his drinking stopped. While their financial situation had improved, the relationship had deteriorated. When Bill asked what the problem was, the wife said, "He's cold, selfish and does not know how to give love." She gave some evidence for her assertions. He was constantly talking on the phone, going out to meetings or coffee with his friends who were recovering from alcohol problems, watching television or reading the paper instead of spending time with her or their child. Her husband agreed that he had been a bit selfish during his drinking years and even currently, as he was absorbed with AA and his recovery. He did not agree that he could not change or that he was cold and incapable of love. In that first session, we did not have time to do much, but Bill got the woman to agree to return and not to proceed with a divorce until they had had at least three sessions of marital therapy.

When they returned, Bill asked how things had gone. The wife said, "I'm past feeling angry at him. I feel sorry for him. He is so wrapped up in himself and so incapable of giving that I'm sure he'll end up a bitter, lonely old man." The husband got very upset upon hearing this opening, as he had really tried to show his wife love during that week. She was amazed at his declaration that he had been putting himself out.

Before they could get into an argument about this, Bill stopped them and asked the husband for one or two examples of what he had done to show his wife love during that week. He said, "Well, take the other day. She came home from work and I was already there. When I saw her coming up the walk with a bag of groceries in her arms, I put down the paper and met her at the door. I carried the groceries into the kitchen and put some of the groceries away. I also cooked vegetables for dinner."

Bill turned to the wife and asked if, indeed, this did not indicate that he was putting himself out and showing her love. She said that she could get a maid to do those things. She wanted a partner who would care for her. The man threw up his hands and said, "See, you can't please her. She's right, maybe we should get a divorce. I'll never be able to do it right!"

Bill turned again to the woman and asked, "What would have looked like love and caring to you in that situation? What could he have done to show you that he loves you?" After some discussion, we found that love would be the man sitting in the kitchen and asking her how her day had been. He was to indicate interest in her day by looking at her (not reading the paper or watching television), nodding his head, and asking follow-up questions to what she told him. We arranged for him to do this for 15 minutes a night, just after she got home. He was amazed at the effect this had on her. She stopped talking about divorce and stopped being so angry at him.

Before he hadn't had any idea what he could do to show her that he loved her. When he tried what he thought looked like love, it didn't work. When we took the time to find out what she thought looked like love, it worked like a charm.

Transcending Maps
of Love

If we keep in mind the idea of unpacking packaged words, we see that an obvious way to encourage being and acting in love again is to find out what is on the spouses' maps of love and have them do those things for each other. A step beyond that is to accept love the way it is given.

Bill's father, Bob, died of cancer when Bill was in his twenties. While Bill was growing up, Bob would often secretly slip Bill a five dollar bill and say, "Here's five dollars; don't tell your mom." Bill's mom thought that his dad was too generous and loose with money. As Bill thought about this later in life, he realized that this was his father's way of saying, "I love you." Bill, as most people, preferred to get his love with an "I love you" and a hug, but realized that this was his father's way of expressing his love. So, every time his father slipped him some money and said, "Don't tell your mother," Bill would translate that into, "I love you, Bill."

When Bob first became ill with cancer, Bill called his dad on the phone. When the conversation came to a close he said, "I just want you to know how much I appreciate all you've done for me as a father. I love you, Dad." Bob replied, rather quickly and dismissively, "Yeah, I love all my kids." Bill just shrugged and again realized his father's discomfort with the direct expression of love. In the third and final year of Bob's fight with cancer, he came to stay in Arizona where Bill was going to college, but after a short time Bob became so ill that he had to return to Nebraska. Bill and his father were at the airport. Both knew that this was probably the last time they would see each other. Bill turned to his father and said, "I love you, Dad." Bob said, "Yeah, I love all my kids." Bill repeated very slowly, while looking Bob in the eyes, "No, Dad, *I love you*." Bob started to cry, they hugged, and Bob said, "I love you."

Bill's father had finally done Bill's map of love yet. Even if Bob had never said, "I love you," Bill would still have known that he loved him. Bill understood that "Here's five dollars don't tell your mom" was love too.

This story has two morals. The first: Realize that the person may be giving love in the only way he or she can or knows how. The therapist can help the partner recognize that love is being expressed. The second: Sometimes people can be taught to express love in different ways, ways that more closely resemble their partner's map.

Sometimes people can use spiritual resources to rise above their petty concerns and maps about love.

Sue and Sean had been referred by their minister for help in dealing with Sean's violence in the marriage. We worked for a time with Sean alone. We found that his spiritual life was very important to him, so we decided to use this in treatment. Every time he felt as if he were losing control, he was able to develop the resource of imagining Christ standing beside him with His hand resting on Sean's shoulder letting His love flow through him. Follow-up several years later indicated that the image had stuck with him and he was able to use it in situations that previously would have led to violence. He was even able to use his spiritual resources in other marital conflicts to help him calm down and feel more loving towards Sue.

Losing Sight of the Big Picture

Sometimes when couples are in the midst of conflict or stuck in unproductive patterns, it seems to us as if they have forgotten the big picture. We tell them to remember that this is a loving relationship, not a boxing match. In this arena, if one of them wins, they both lose.

Bill tells a story that has the dual purpose of helping people remember to use caring voice tones and inspiring them to focus on love:

> He had just finished work after a particularly inspirational session with a couple. These spouses had been really mean and nasty to one another when they first came in, but they reached a point in the session when they had cried, told each other how much they loved each other, and made a commitment to be more loving in the future. On the way home Bill stopped at the grocery store to pick up a few items. He had just turned the corner of an aisle and saw a couple in the midst of an argument. The husband was starting to place a box of cereal in the shopping cart when the wife snarled, "I told you we already have that!" When they saw Bill they looked a little embarrassed. He thought to himself, "I bet that if I had a chance to work with them they would say that they love each other, but I'll bet the love did not come across on that channel."

It seems that we save our meanest and most critical tones for the people whom we love the most. We try to help spouses remember that they came together out of love. Love can help people rise above the petty quarrels of life. We want to remind people to act in a way that is consistent with that love.

Relationship Wimps and Big Bowls: Making Relationships Last

Since we want to make a lasting difference and since staying together for the long run is a challenge for many couples today, we have investigated what makes relationships last. We try to impart some of those ideas and principles to our clients. We sometimes tell clients stories that will help them make their relationships last.

Pat was working with Michelle and Sam. They had been married for over 20 years and had two college-age sons. Sam had had a brief affair but Michelle had not found out about it until it had been over for a few months. It was hard for Sam to get very interested in even talking about the affair since it was, in his mind, over and done with. Nevertheless, it became clear in the course of the therapy that Sam was barely committed to the marriage. Pat told a story from our relationship.

Pat said, "When Bill and I were dating we had a disagreement about getting together with his family. He had made arrangements to get together with them at a time when, if the starting of the get-together had been delayed 20 or 30 minutes, I could have joined them too. I was hurt that Bill did not consider this and, at the time, I was discouraged about all the adjustments that seemed necessary for us to go through to maintain our relationship. When Bill came home from the family get-together, I said that I thought we should break up. It was just too hard there were too many people involved—my three kids, his big family (he is one of eight kids) and it just seemed too overwhelming. After we negotiated the issue that had led to my being upset and made some future agreements about his making an effort to include me in social plans, Bill asked me if I was a relationship wimp. I said, 'I don't know, what is a "relationship wimp"?' He said, 'A relationship wimp is someone who cannot handle any strain in the relationship. I want you to exercise that relationship muscle and be able to work through these little things with me so that you will be strong and can make it through the big things that will surely come along.' A couple of years later I gave the same speech to Bill and told him I wanted him to have the courage to make the relationship what he wanted it to be."

Years later, Sam reported that hearing this story was a very important component to his staying in the marriage. He said it helped him make it through a boring stage of his marriage and create a lively and lasting relationship.

Bill was once at a party where there was an older couple who seemed to really enjoy each other and have a lively relationship. They had been married over 50 years. Bill got a chance to talk to the woman alone and told her that he was a therapist, studying how people make their marriages last. He had noticed how lively and positive her marriage seemed to be and he wondered what their secret was. She answered, "I was married to five different men!"

Bill was shocked. He said, "Do you mean that you had four other husbands before you found this one?"

She said, "No. It just seemed like I did. When I married him, he was a lively, handsome, trim young man with idealistic dreams. Then he changed into a man focused intensely on work and making a living. He was like a different man. I did not love that new man at first but I learned to love him. Just when it seemed I'd gotten used to this new one, he changed again. He went through what's called today a 'mid-life crisis,' only we didn't know about those in those days. He became disinterested in work, dissatisfied and disillusioned about being the breadwinner and all of that, and I had to learn to love him all over again in that stage. Then he came out of that and settled into his older years. Now he has a wisdom and depth I really appreciate, but look over there. [She pointed to her husband.] That doesn't look like the man I married—this one has saggy skin and a bit of a pot belly—but I have learned to love that man in that saggy body too."

Her story inspires us and we have used it to inspire our couples. Love has a quality of being a choice and choosing to learn to love a person as he or she changes seems to be part of making a long-term marriage lively and caring.

We were working with Don and Kara. They both said that they were not sure if they still loved each other. We told them that one thing psychology has shown is that, if you do actions, feelings consistent with those actions often follow. We found out from assertiveness training that, if you do assertive behaviors, you will start to feel assertive. If one starts acting loving, then feelings of love may follow. We suggested that they ask themselves, "If this was the love of my life, how would I treat him or her? How would I talk to him when we come home from work today? How would I touch her? What actions can I take that would communicate my love and caring?" This was

a turning point for Don and Kara. This was just the
push in the direction they needed.

How Big Is Your Bowl?

One of the skills in making a relationship last, then, is to
stay through the tough and discouraging times. We use
the analogy of a bowl. The size of your bowl determines
how long you stay in the relationship. The bigger the
bowl, the more it can contain, the longer you stay.

When you first meet someone as a friend or partner,
your bowl may be pretty small. Almost anything the person does that you don't like or that you get upset about
can fall outside the bowl. Maybe they forget a breakfast
date with you. You may decide to forget the relationship,
because you hate being stood up or you felt too humiliated
waiting alone in the restaurant. If so, forgetting a breakfast
date fell outside your bowl of relationship. If you decide
to carry on with the relationship, however, your bowl has
just grown a bit bigger. Then you have your first argument. You may decide that the relationship is too conflic-
tual or that you just aren't compatible. If so, the bowl is
small. If you decide to stay and work it out, the bowl gets
bigger. If it gets big enough to handle anything, then the
relationship will last.

We have seen couples make it through things that have
severed other relationships: affairs, long separations,
physical violence, long-term ill health of one of the partners, the death of one of their children. These people have
big bowls that can contain whatever happens within the
context of their relationship.

Now when we are talking about the bowl, we don't
mean to imply that couples should just stay together and
be miserable. That is not a great model for satisfying, lov-

ing relationships. We have also seen the instant divorces and serial marriages that indicate little tolerance for frustration and little commitment. We are searching for some middle ground here. We encourage couples not to stay together and be miserable, but to work actively on making their relationships satisfying while staying through the times when they feel discouraged.

Pat Hudson's Four Relationship Principles

When Pat went through her divorce she devoted many hours, often in the middle of the night, to thinking about why some relationships last and others don't. She concluded that it takes four factors to make a good lasting relationship: skills, ethics, commitment, and a sense of humor.

The first part of this book spoke about the skills part: getting couples to communicate clearly what they like and don't like about each others' actions in the relationship getting them to interact without blaming, invalidating, or closing down possibilities. We work actively to validate and acknowledge each person's experience and to get him or her to stop trying to change the other's basic nature.

We spoke about ethics in Chapter 8 on dealing with soap-opera-like lapses and destructive actions in the relationship.

In this chapter, we have detailed our thoughts on commitment and sticking through the difficult times in relationships.

We hope that we have modeled the use of humor throughout the book, as well as in Chapter 7, which dealt specifically with the topic.

In a way, these are the principles that serve to make good therapy as well: Develop your therapeutic skills, treat people ethically (respecting boundaries and confidentiality), stay committed to your clients and to results, and keep your sense of humor. We hope this book has contributed to all those areas in your work with couples.

REFERENCES

Bateson, Mary Catherine. (1989). *Composing a Life*. New York: Plume.

Carl, Douglas. (1990). *Counseling Same-Sex Couples*. New York: Norton.

Gleick, J. (1987). *Chaos: Making a New Science*. New York: Viking.

Hudson, R. Lofton. (1963). *Marital Counseling*. Englewood Cliffs, NJ: Prentice-Hall.

Imber-Black, Evan, Roberts, Janine, and Whiting, Richard (Eds.). (1988). *Rituals in Families and Family Therapy*. New York: Norton.

Jacobs, Jane, and Wolin, George. (1989). Ritual Strengthening. *Family Therapy Networker, 13*:4, 41, July/August.

Newhorn, Paula. (1973). *Primal Sensuality: New Discoveries in the Enjoyment of Sex*. Greenwich, CT: Fawcett Crest.

O'Hanlon, Bill, and Wilk, James. (1987). *Shifting Contexts: The Generation of Effective Psychotherapy*. New York: Guilford.

O'Hanlon, William H. (1987). *Taproots: Underlying Principles of Milton H. Erickson's Therapy and Hypnosis*. New York: Norton.

O'Hanlon, William H., and Weiner-Davis, Michele. (1989). *In Search of Solutions: A New Direction in Psychotherapy*. New York: Norton.

O'Hanlon, William H., and Martin, Michael S. (In press). *A Brief Guide to Solution-Oriented Hypnosis*. New York: Norton.

Van der Hart, Onno. (1983). *Rituals in Psychotherapy: Transition and Continuity*. New York: Irvington.

Weiner-Davis, Michele. (1987). On Being an Unabashed Marriage Saver. *Family Therapy Networker, 11*:1, 53–56, January/February.

Winograd, Terry, and Flores, Fernando. (1987). *Understanding Computers and Cognition*. Reading, MA: Addison-Wesley.

INDEX